10-4-65

STRUGGLE OF DECENCY

159

STRUGGLE
OF DECENCY

RELIGION AND RACE
IN MODERN AMERICA

Robert Root and Shirley W. Hall

FRIENDSHIP PRESS   NEW YORK

LIBRARY OF CONGRESS CATALOG CARD NUMBER: 65-11440

To

*Joshua and Christopher Hall
and
Ed, Marilyn and Carol Root
. . . hopefully*

CONTENTS

Preface

The writers of this book claim some kind of first, since we know no other study such as this which has been done by "integrated authorship." We have enjoyed the exchanges which have come in the blending of Negro and white viewpoints, and what emerges is our common voice in duet. However, since the white majority is often unclear on Negro attitudes, there are some things which need to be said frankly from the Negro point of view, and Mrs. Hall has said them; these are set off in italics to indicate that they are the ideas of one young Negro mother and journalist, but they are nonetheless a part of our common presentation.

The "struggle of decency" as it emerges against bigotry and intolerance is also a struggle *for* decency in neighbors' treatment of neighbors. If there is a special justification for this book when so much is being written about race relations, it is that it focuses on the religious forces working for interracial brotherhood. We look at the race question from the perspective of the churches, especially the Protestant churches of America. We have tried to show where and how Christians have aided the struggle for decency in such areas as accommodations and education but also within their own organizations. In this sense it follows up that too optimistically-titled book, *Progress Against Prejudice,* written by one of us. The events here reported make clear that there has been advance since Friendship Press published that one in 1957, but we prefer the present emphasis on continuing struggle.

Finally we wish to express our appreciation to the editors and others who have helped us with ideas and criticisms, and especially to Christine V. Root for her advice and assistance.

ROBERT ROOT
SHIRLEY W. HALL

Syracuse, New York

PART ONE

DECENCY AND INDIGNITY

Prologue: On Being a Negro

> Racial segregation creates conflicts in self-esteem and deep feelings of inferiority in Negro youth. It depresses their motivation, constricts their perspective and lowers their educational and vocational aspiration.
> —Kenneth Clark

White people go whole days without thinking about the race problem. Negroes cannot. And every Negro has had experiences with his Negro-ness that have shaped his whole view of life. For example:

At age ten I found out I was a Negro.[1]

We lived in a white community—integrated, if you call it that when there are one or two Negro families who settle in a place long before it is a town. We were "accepted" to a fair degree. We went to school with white kids and had white friends.

Our community happened to be the residence of a man who ran bingo games, and all the proceeds on Friday nights went to our Girl Scouts. We were a rich troop. Our uniforms were paid for, and our camping too. This was probably the main reason that I could go to camp.

[1] This and other sections in italics represent Mrs. Hall's personal comments from a Negro viewpoint, as explained in the preface.

I was fortunate to have "poor but honest," hardworking, God-fearing parents. My father was a post office clerk. Each family had only to assume the responsibility for getting its daughter to the camp, located some twenty miles from the town.

When we arrived we were greeted by a camp counselor who said, "May I have your name? Oh, yes . . . please wait one moment. The camp director will be over to speak to you."

How lovely, we thought, the camp director takes time to greet everybody!

The director came quickly. She didn't offer to shake hands but looked directly at my father and said, "Mr. Wiley, we do not allow Negro girls at this camp."

I wondered immediately what the other girls would think. To me there was a stigma attached to my rejection which put the onus on me, not on the people doing the rejecting. To my ten-year-old mind, not letting me stay indicated something was wrong with me.

Maybe the other girls had known this all along, and here I had been forcing myself on them, assuming myself to be their equal! Embarrassment churned inside me—the way one might feel on realizing after a successful speech that some part of her attire was in disarray and the audience knew it all the time.

Even today, I find that when I run into prejudice, my first response is to feel rejection because I am unworthy. Later I am able to be intelligent about it and realize that I am more sinned against than sinner, but the pain is still there.

When you are rejected because of race, you don't think. "It is he who is bad, not me." You just don't think that way. You remember other little incidents—the girls in your class brushing their skin off because you accidentally touched them—the rest of history class turning to look at

*you when slavery is discussed—the birthday party to which
everybody in your class was invited but you.*

So at camp in this awful moment, I cried. Nor did it assuage my feelings any that my father—so angry that his
voice came out in a hoarse whisper—was saying to the director, "It so happens that I publish a weekly newspaper, and
I will fight this thing if it's the last thing I do!"

I cried all the way back home. My younger brothers
were in the car and they cried—mostly, I think, because I
was crying. But who is to say what traumatic impression
this made on their minds, since both are now active in the
civil rights movement?

My father wouldn't speak to anyone on the way back.
Mom had to drive, try to console three children hurt by a
force she was powerless to stop. At home Dad shut the
bedroom door and opened the portable typewriter. That
week's "Chronicle" had banner headlines:

SCOUT CAMP REFUSES NEGRO GIRL

On the front page also was Dad's caustic editorial, "Con-
sistency Is Indeed a Jewel." The camp board of directors
had disregarded one of the laws which form the foundation
of Girl Scouting: "A Girl Scout is a friend to all and a sister
to every other Girl Scout." They had acted, they said, from
"honest" motives—but because of them, a Negro girl was
friendless and lonely.

How it feels to be a Negro today can be boiled down to
two words: ego damage. In the words of James Baldwin:
"The Negro child . . . looking at the society that has produced him . . . understands that this structure is operated
for someone else's benefit—not for his."

Why should a Negro youngster, surrounded in his ghetto
by hundreds of other dark-skinned people, assume that, be-

cause he sees one or two Negroes with a decent job, he too can achieve? His decision must be to become exceptional, for only then can he perhaps live as an average white person.

Dr. Kenneth Clark, the Negro psychologist who drafted ideas used in the 1954 Supreme Court decision on integration of schools, has pointed out how Negro youngsters have such "a general sense of hopelessness and despair" that they adopt protective devices in a pathetic attempt to make their lives tolerable. These devices include withdrawal and dropping out of school.

In Harlem, Dr. Clark has been a prime mover of HARYOU (Harlem Youth Opportunities Unlimited). Its aim is to overcome ego damage with a program helping young people to work for social change themselves and so to increase their "sense of pride, confidence and initiative."

Concerned, thinking Christians must support such efforts to reclaim both Negro youth and older Negroes whose personality has suffered. These programs must be undertaken in an attitude of love but not condescension.

One of the hardest realities to be faced by many whites who would like to help is that while they can—must—give money and support, many Negroes cannot or will not relate to them, at least not in the beginning. Negroes must be the administrators. Otherwise special projects will only reinforce the notion that even when Negroes are in positions of authority, there are always whites who are over them.

1 · Golden Rule or Backlash

> What the world expects of Christians is that Christians should speak out loud and clear.
>
> —Albert Camus

In part it's a question of imagination.

Imagine a little boy, an American boy. The world has plenty of worries, but as he grows up, we see a great future for him nevertheless. He'll get a good education, then a good job; he'll marry and have a fine family—and, yes, he might even be president! That's still the American dream for little American boys.

But as a recent expression puts it: *Color him black.* The dream changes. There are happy exceptions, but if we're honest, we know that the "typical" or "average" picture for the little Negro boy is this:

He may not go hungry, but he'll eat a poor family's diet. His house—or perhaps an overcrowded flat—will be run-down and drafty. He'll go to school, but the school in his neighborhood won't be as good as in the white suburbs. He'll have more diseases, statistically speaking.

In the cities, North and South, he'll see more than his share of moral derelicts of both races around him—petty thieves, drunks, dope addicts, prostitutes. He'll learn soon enough that if his parents had the money to move—and they don't—they wouldn't be accepted in the fine white neighborhoods with the fine white schools. And he'll learn, too, that it will not be easy, may be impossible, for him ever to get a better job than those held by his father and his friends—the bellhops, garbage collectors, ditch diggers, broompushers of the slum.

Why try for college, or even high school, if that's the future? The Negro boy's dreams shrivel, and he drops out of school to take a job, any unskilled job, even without a future. Maybe he gets a bright, shiny car he can race, or cuts up with some musical "cats" or a similarly frustrated girl who wants some fun before she settles down to being a cleaning woman. Maybe he throws rocks or shoots guns, out of his resentment and frustration and hate.

The well-meaning white man looks with disgust at this Negro boy's sloth. And if that white man is particularly lacking in imagination, he'll say: "A good for nothin', lazy fella like that doesn't deserve to mix with white folks. The Negro won't get equality till he deserves it. He ought to go out and get a good job and make something of himself."

Out of a background like that? With horizons that the whites have tightened in on the typical black boy?

This isn't to excuse the Negro. He *should* go to school, and he *should* save his money and improve his home, and he *should* attend church. Many Negroes do. But is it realistic to expect that, if environment is squalid and hopeless, the majority of people, of any race, will do that? Can a man lift himself by his bootstraps unless someone else is tugging up on them too, whether he is poor white or Arab or Asian or Negro? And what happens to the person who could help but turns his head?

Every day, continuously and persistently, life reminds a Negro that his status in America is inferior.

The day begins in a house which is a reminder. Few Negroes can be selective about their residences. Even when a Negro is fortunate enough to have the resources to move to a middle-income section of the city, he cannot select his home from all those that are on the market, but only from those whose owners will show to him. So even a move to an "integrated" neighborhood has frustrations in terms of his dreams.

If there is a child, any parental reflections about him during the day have an added dimension: How will his being Negro affect his chances? How can I help him to tolerate less understanding people and at the same time accept the challenge to remove bigotry?

The workday begins. There are many reminders here that the Negro is last hired and first fired. Few of his race get the promotions to foreman. In thousands of business establishments, Negroes are hired only in maintenance and manual work.

Perhaps during the day a Negro mother and her child will be shopping or riding a bus. It is still not infrequent for a five-year old white child to comment loudly to his parent, "Mama, there's a black baby," or "Don't let that little boy touch me—his skin is all dirty!" The white parent is usually embarrassed and tries to shush the child or move him quickly away. The Negro mother feels pain inside at this evidence that many white children are being brought up with so little contact with Negroes that they believe dark-skinned people are "dirty." She wishes whites would have the decency to apologize for their offspring's bad manners and to explain to them, in front of the Negro family and with their help, about the various colors of people in America and the world.

The day may have in it an incident at school, where the children face up to race and its caste implications.

Kevin, a real ten-year old, is the only Negro in his classroom. The teacher became ill, and no one had told the substitute that Kevin had joined the group several weeks late. So having a substitute was harder on Kevin than the others. The substitute often had the children choose sides in playing games, and Kevin was always the last one selected. His mother suggested that perhaps it was his newness to the group. But Kevin, who was having the experience of being called race names as he walked home from school, could not believe this.

The day of the Negro may also bring a warming experience related to his Negritude, and I shall mention one here —but not so people can sweetly comment, "But aren't we making wonderful progress?"

One of the boys who used to jeer at Kevin found that he could add to the discomfort by walking close to his heels as he shouted names. Since Kevin's mother works—few Negroes can afford the luxury of staying home with their children—Kevin had no one at home to serve as a buffer; but fortunately Joe, a white boy Kevin had become friendly with at school, told her what was happening. In aroused indignation she called the principal. The principal had the offending child report to her office, and after talking with him called Kevin's mother at work.

"I am sorry to learn of how Kevin has been treated," she said. "You can be sure that we are taking steps to see that such behavior does not take place on the school grounds or in the classrooms." She indicated that she was also keeping Winton after school for a week in an effort to improve his attitude even away from school.

This conversation gave Kevin's mother a chance to mention his difficulty because of the substitute. Here again was a matter the principal could act on forthrightly, and she did. Now the situation became a learning experience for *pupils, their parents, the substitute, and the regular teacher on her return.*

Kevin learned a valuable lesson, too—that to have a friend, he had to be one, perhaps extending himself somewhat. By the end of the school year he had become, according to his teachers, one of the most popular children in the school.

Those of us who are white can't *feel* how it is to be black in a society dominated by whites—our imaginations sustain us for only a few pages, a handful of moments, if that long. Our failure is perhaps not so much of conscience as of imagination. The white community does not practice the Golden Rule toward the Negro because it does not try hard enough to sense how the Negro is "done unto" and would want to be done unto.

Howard Griffin, a white man who colored his skin and later wrote *Black Like Me*, says that when he was "a Negro" he developed "an awful sense of dread at the beginning of every day."

If whites could *know* in terms of actual experience the bitter injustices practiced against those who are black, perhaps conscience would drive them to do more than they do to right wrongs. There are of course some white Americans who do not want or pretend to be brotherly. When they talk about freedom, they are claiming some constitutional right to be unfair. They demand the freedom to treat human beings worse than animals—for whoever heard of burning the cross on the lawn of the Society for the Prevention of Cruelty to Animals? They want to be free to keep minority peoples in menial jobs and in slums. To them American liberty does not mean freedom for Negroes to fight for decent jobs and decent homes; somehow that struggle is a radical, "foreign" idea.

The major sin, however, is not willful unkindness, but silence. Most of America's privileged, which includes the majority of whites and perhaps a few Negroes, do not cry out against racial injustice because they do not feel what that injustice means to Negroes. They are short on compassion. We who are white are calloused.

"There is a shocking lack of empathy on the part of the white person to the plight of the Negro," the chairman of the New York State Commission for Human Rights, George H. Fowler, said recently in assessing this phenomenon. "The white person has not placed himself in the position of the Negro or other victims of bias. The white person, therefore, in many instances is ill equipped to understand what's happening today in the grass-roots protests manifested by the sit-ins, stand-ins, peaceful picketing and other public demonstrations of a disillusioned, frustrated and almost desperate people."

In an interview not long ago, the Negro writer John Oliver Killens made a similar point. The white man's failure to comprehend powerful Negro emotions today is responsible for an explosive danger in the race struggle, he said, and Negro intellectuals must explain this to white colleagues.

"The Negro artists, like the Negro people, are becoming more and more disillusioned with white America," the Georgia-born novelist went on. "The disillusionment of the Negro people is today reflected in the works of the Negro artists. They speak for the people who are inarticulate. You can push men so far and then they will strike back."

The Indians have a proverb, "Don't criticize another person until you have walked from sun up to sun up in his moccasins."

One of the main values of having Negroes and whites continue to meet, of "keeping the lines of communication open," is that imaginations can be sharpened, feelings conveyed.

Our area Council of Churches sponsored a workshop, and a professor of sociology who chaired our group opened by asking, "To what extent is there a communication flow from the Negro community to the white and from the white community to the Negro?"

There was silence as the question was pondered.

"I really don't think this race prejudice thing is so important, not in the North, anyway."

"Negroes really aren't so bad off. Look at the American Indian. He has fewer rights than the Negro."

"I don't see color when I choose my friends. Some of my best friends are Negroes."

And so on.

Negroes hear these statements from well-meaning, "concerned" white people nearly every day. It's one of the occupational handicaps of being a Negro. It is also part of the pain.

An opportunity was about to slip by. Twenty-five workshop participants would go to their homes certain that they had made a worthwhile contribution to better race relations.

"It's a pity more Negroes didn't attend the meeting. How can we communicate with them if they don't come? We white people are here."

This last from a little old lady who up to now had not talked up.

Most of us four Negroes hadn't yet spoken, for we tend to let white persons talk on and on, convinced of their own liberality. But after a while the point is reached where the Negro section of any biracial discussion feels duty-bound to try to interpret, correct, or otherwise guide the whites into some sharper insights.

That is why, that "point of no return" now reached, we opened up.

"You may not realize it, but you have answered the opening question. There is little, if any, communication from Negroes to whites. White people don't know what it is like to be a Negro, although it is clear and obvious to Negroes what it's like to be white."

Workshop time was beginning to run out, but white mouths dropped and eyes saucered as Negroes volunteered:

"If white people were suddenly to have to live for twenty-four hours under the discrimination that daily plagues the Negro all his life, they would crack up."

"Do you know why there aren't more Negroes present? Because the Negroes figure that they have had enough of these once-a-year, 'Christian social concern', go-go brotherhood affairs. When the celebration is over, whites can wrap their brotherhood in tissue paper and put it back on the shelf for another year."

"There's more prejudice and discrimination in the North than in the South." Utter disbelief. "Surely not here?"

The bell ending the workshop sounded, but not before general agreement had been reached that the openness of the discussion had brought new insights. "Can't we keep on meeting? We want to hear more—do more."

The Communications Workshop met four times after that. There was more sharing, learning, giving and taking, and one opportunity for real action. The evening newspaper had published a series of anti-civil rights editorials. Workshop members took to the streets with 10,000 leaflets answering them.

To point up the lack of imagination by the white is not to excuse the Negro when he doesn't use his head. He is a human being and subject to the same errors as the white man—and it is just as far from the truth for him to generalize that all whites are hypocrites as for the white to generalize that all Negroes are musical. The Negro has great provocation to conclude that all whites are evil, as the Jews did to conclude that all Germans were, but his humanness demands that he try to find humanity even among the whites.

It is on the white man, of course, that the burden of responsibility and guilt falls most heavily. The late French writer Camus, quoted at the beginning of this section from his *Resistance, Rebellion and Death,* was an existentialist who called himself an "unbeliever," so his critique is especially cutting when he says that the world expects the Christian to speak out clearly against injustice. That Christian voice has not been so loud or clear as it should on the race issue.

Far from leading, says one American clergyman who was a Freedom Rider, "the church isn't even following any more." That overstates the case. Churchmen are helping some phases of the race struggle, as numerous illustrations in this book will demonstrate.

Whenever one approaches praise of American white Christians, however, he must speak with restraint, for so much more is still to be done. The sins of omission remain great. Dean Heinrich Grüber of West Berlin put it in an address not long ago. A German Lutheran leader, he was one clergyman who tried to save Jews from Nazi persecution during World War II. As if echoing Camus, he asserted that the deaths of millions of Jews would not have to be mourned if thousands of German churchmen and other leaders had protested "loudly and publicly." But turning to American racism, he declared: "Formerly, I was ashamed to be a German, but after my visit to the United States, I am ashamed to be white."

If the shame is greater in our South, the Northern white

has no reason to feel self-righteous. If he will imagine himself a Negro and open his Negro eyes to the world about him, he will see that Northern society too is a white society which either subordinates or excludes minority peoples. In the society pages of his newspapers and in the ads, how often does he see a Negro bride or a Negro model? Sometimes, but rarely. How often does a brown manikin display fashions in the store windows? In early 1964, the businessmen of our Northern city claimed to be the first in the United States to order Negro manikins. Fashionable Bergdorf-Goodman on New York's Fifth Avenue used two Negro manikins in a back-to-school display in August, 1964.

Even on television, in spite of the Negroes' great reputation as entertainers, there are white barriers. Negro stars have been confined to guest appearances. Nat (King) Cole had a weekly show on NBC but couldn't get a sponsor. Not long before his death he said TV is opening up and he was looking forward to a series of his own specials. "I think it will come—in time," said Mr. Cole.

In 1963 the Protestant Council of the City of New York appealed to the television industry and advertisers to include Negroes in programs and commercials. Another approach was made by the Protestants who petitioned the Federal Communications Commission to deny reissue of a TV license to a Mississippi station which allegedly ignored Negro news, church services, and other activities.

For years the Negro was told, although not in so many words, that he wasn't part of America. The people pictured in advertisements, enjoying jam, cookies, ice cream, cosmetics, and so on, were always white. So were the characters in the fiction in most magazines.

When he turned to a Negro publication, he would find that, when his dollar was involved, advertisers would spend money to hire Negro models to convince him to buy. Earliest pressure to change this came from groups that insisted Negroes should be given roles similar to those they had in our society. As the civil rights demonstrations have grown, Negroes have appeared in more and more stories, books, advertisements, TV dramas and commercials.

Even now, however, the situation comedies on TV never have characters come into close contact with Negroes, as neighbors, classmates, or members of their church. Why couldn't one of the family entertainment shows spoof the "problems" of a Negro family moving into the neighborhood?

If you're a Negro, what motel do you stop at? Life is a constant embarrassing test of rights, even if you're mild as a mouse. Where do you get a haircut? On a national TV show, an African student told of his embarrassment (and America's embarrassment) when a barber refused to cut his hair—not in South Carolina but in South Dakota! In Madison, New Jersey, a group picketed barber shops where Negroes were refused. Later, six Negroes and six white faculty members of Drew University tried to get haircuts in that city, and the university chaplain was arrested for "disorderly conduct." Two hundred white persons cheered as police made the arrest!

Packaging is another area in which the Negro is still invisible. Roll your cart through the aisles of any supermarket and pick up a package of everything with a human face on it. You will have baby cereal with a loving mother (white Anglo-Saxon) holding her child; an assortment of baby foods with pink babies. Why not advertise the diversity that is America—at the same time indicating the similarities in mother love, baby appeal and cleanliness—with packages

showing mothers of all races holding their babies to their
bosoms? It would be worth the extra investment for models
to help minority children develop feelings of worth.

The civil rights movement has cut away a great deal of
hypocrisy and brought anti-Negro feelings out more sharply.
Everyone is aware of the concessions that are made to hard-
core resistance to integration. Even the liberal white, reading of incidents in which segregationists have "won out," is
inclined to view them merely as touchdowns for the opposition. For the Negro, who is more involved personally, they
are an affront and discouragement.

White plumbers in New York refused to work with
Negroes and Puerto Ricans on a Bronx project. For many
whites it was disappointing—for Negroes it was another insult. Near San Francisco, Curt Flood, Negro center fielder
of the world champion St. Louis Cardinals, had to sue in
1964 to live in a suburban home he had leased. For whites,
that demonstrated "we still have a long way to go"—for
Negroes it seemed another backhand to the cheek.

The popularity of the segregationist Governor George C.
Wallace of Alabama during the "backlash" against civil
rights was not lost on Negroes. Governor Wallace, who
"stood in the door" to try to prevent integration of the University of Alabama, is a "good" man. A Methodist, he did
not campaign on Sundays, and for many years he taught
Sunday school in his home town.

Leaders of a number of denominations in various areas
publicly assailed the Wallace ideas, and that heartened
many, whites and Negroes alike. Still, for Negroes, the fact
that Wallace was able to get a following was simply another
bitter proof of how bigoted whites are.

The pervasive prejudices smoked out by agitation and
demonstration have brought one overall reaction by Ne-

groes. General protest has come in response to general discrimination. From specific complaints the Negro pressure has moved on to "revolution."

"What the white people do not understand is that the protest has now moved from the lunch counters in 1960 to the general approach," a Negro leader explained in Nashville in May, 1964. "We must now maintain pressure against towns that have sat back and taken pride in the little steps they have made."

The Negro leader who made that comment was the Rev. J. Metz Rollins, one of the staff of the United Presbyterian Church in Philadelphia. Days later 150 religious leaders staged a march at Nashville for "total desegregation."

"You don't have to have any specific objectives," Mr. Rollins explained. "This is a protest against being a Negro in this country."

The Rev. C. T. Vivian of Atlanta, a director of the Southern Christian Leadership Conference, put the same idea this way: "We must be more radical than we were yesterday. That means we are going to have to move more massively and in such ways that we can be heard."

In Harlem, weeks before the 1964 rioting, Negro young people began militant protests. Preaching in this Negro section, the moderator of the New York Presbytery, a Negro, the Rev. Dr. Eugene S. Callender, backed them up: "These kids in Harlem are tired of being trampled on. They do not trust the white man any more. . . . We middle class Negroes, living in comfortable apartments, mixing with our own group of friends both white and colored, have not been aware of the feelings of the masses. These kids are starting to get those feelings across to us—and we had better listen now."

So the Negro reaction to white insensitivity and callousness has been growing restiveness and belligerence, to get all civil rights clean across the board, and NOW.

PART TWO

TEST OF DEMOCRACY—STILL

2 · Challenge of Status: Accommodations

> We have come now to a kind of testing. We must not
> fail. Let us close the springs of racial poison. Let us
> pray for wise and understanding hearts. Let us lay
> aside irrelevant differences and make our nation whole.
> Let us hasten that day when our unbounded spirit will
> be free to do the great works ordained for this nation
> by the just and wise God who is the Father of all.
> —Lyndon B. Johnson, in signing
> the 1964 civil rights bill

There must have been a slip-up. When the Rev.
Dr. Jesse Barber, a United Presbyterian churchman from
New York, presented his confirmed reservation at the exclusive Columbia Club in downtown Indianapolis, it was
not honored.

He was in the city for the General Assembly of his church,
since he was assistant secretary of the Division of Evangel-
ism, Board of National Missions. He was also a former dean
of Lincoln Theological Seminary in Pennsylvania. But no
matter. He was a Negro.

For years Presbyterians had been passing resolutions.
Here was a concrete incident. What would they do? They
moved quickly to invoke a standing rule against racial discrimination, and sixty delegates moved out of the club. "The
quick action by church officials was praised by many

delegates as a courageous step that put into practice what the church had been preaching for many years," wrote the *New York Times'* religion editor, George Dugan.

That was in 1959, five years before the civil rights law barred discrimination in public accommodations. For years changes in custom had been coming under the stimulus of protests like the one in Indianapolis, sometimes with a push from state laws. In one Northern city, an economics professor led a lunch-counter demonstration in the early forties to get a chain drug store to integrate—two decades before the Congress of Racial Equality (CORE) made such demonstrations a commonplace.

Not long after the Indianapolis incident, and not very far away, students at Fisk in Nashville—a Negro university with some white students—started a push to get lunch counters to serve Negroes.

"This is no student panty raid," explained the Fisk president, Stephen J. Wright. "It is a dedicated universal effort."

First the students tried lunch-counter sit-ins. Massive arrests followed. Nashville's mayor appointed a biracial committee that worked out a ninety-day test of integrated counters. That failed.

So then the students started "hit-and-run" sit-ins. When a counter closed rather than serve Negroes, the students did not sit-in but left. Then as soon as it opened, they came back. This technique, of course, could keep a counter closed most of the time.

Then at Easter, 1960, elders joined in. Negroes withdrew their estimated $7.5 million annual patronage from downtown stores. This hurt, since they account for 15 percent or more of the business of Nashville department and variety stores.

Within Protestantism, national attention now centered on a young divinity student at Vanderbilt University. A 31-

year old Negro and Methodist minister, the Rev. James M.
Lawson, Jr. had spent three years in India as a missionary.
He was a strong believer in nonviolent resistance and helped
train a cadre of about a hundred of the students to practice
this technique in the face of violent provocation. Like
Gandhi, he took the view that if necessary, sit-in demonstrators should break the law in order to bring about
integration.

The Vanderbilt chancellor tried to get him to renounce
this view. He wouldn't, so the chancellor dismissed him
from the university. The Vanderbilt board backed up the
decision, and the young Methodist left for Boston University.

The action of the board stirred sharp dissent among the
professors. Dr. Robert J. Nelson, dean of the divinity school,
and ten faculty members resigned. Several of them later
went back when a plan was worked out for Mr. Lawson to
get a degree without reentering. But Dr. Nelson, a graduate
of DePauw University and Yale Divinity School, held to his
resignation and later accepted a position as professor of
ecumenics at Princeton Theological Seminary.

The upshot was that integration came to Nashville public
accommodations, except among a few holdouts.

Around the nation all through 1960, segregation of eating
facilities—symbolized by the lunch counter—broke down.

In San Antonio, Texas, the counters were integrated without incident under the leadership of a 17-year-old college
freshman girl and the executive director of the city's council
of churches. Fortuitously, the change was climaxed by an
interracial, interfaith banquet, which had been planned for
four months by two predominantly Negro churches, Second
Baptist and St. Paul Methodist.

Galveston, Texas, shortly afterward became the second
Texas city to integrate its counters. The step was taken

voluntarily after a conference of business leaders with Protestant, Catholic and Jewish representatives.

At Miami, Florida, downtown counters were integrated without incident that summer. "It has been handled very quietly," said one interracial leader, the Rev. John E. Culmer, Episcopalian, "and that is how it should be."

In the early spring of 1961, a pastor of the late President Kennedy, the Rev. Albert F. Pereira, served as arbitrator in negotiations as three lunch counters in Middleburg, Virginia, were integrated. Sit-in demonstrations had been planned to coincide with the President's visit there on a Lenten Sunday. Instead, the priest was able to read a prayer, as the President listened: "Eastertide is a time for joy, joy in our unity by baptism in Christ. Hence it is so appropriate that we rejoice today that the first bridge of understanding between the races has been crossed gracefully."

The year 1961 was marked by many other events of success or struggle at eating places, including:

Atlanta, Georgia—Eight ministers and seventy-seven students were jailed in counter sit-ins rather than pay fines under an anti-trespass law. Said the ministers: "We hope to help create righteous indignation in the hearts and minds of the people against discrimination and segregation."

Savannah, Georgia—Bishop Albert R. Stuart of the Episcopal Diocese of Georgia announced agreement on integration of counters after a fifteen-month Negro boycott.

Dallas, Texas—Without publicity, thirty-six restaurants and cafeterias, including the Zodiac Room at Neiman-Marcus, the fashionable department store, were integrated all at once by arrangement of the Dallas Citizens Council (which after the assassination of President Kennedy was to draw critical attention as embodying the city's power structure). A total of 159 Negro business and professional men, clergymen and their wives undertook the planned dining.

Baltimore, Maryland—Integrationists met at the Cornerstone Baptist Church to plan demonstrations at restaurants in Baltimore and Annapolis. Thirty-three were later arrested, including their chairman, the Rev. Logan Kearse of Cornerstone Church.

Efforts to integrate lunch counters at Rock Hill, South Carolina, a textile manufacturing town of 33,000, extended over both 1960 and 1961. One leader was the Rev. C. A. Ivory, a crippled Negro minister confined to a wheelchair. He participated in the sit-ins in spite of his handicap and received threatening phone calls. Finally he was arrested. Wheeling him to jail, shaking him down for weapons and booking him proved awkward. He was released on bail.

The campaign slowed up in the summer. Then Thomas Gaither arrived as CORE field secretary, and sit-ins were started again in the winter. Here are the highlights as he recounts them:

A counter sit-in was planned, though it was known that this would inevitably lead to a jail-in. When the demonstrators entered McCrory's store, they were quickly arrested and charged with trespassing. The judge sentenced them to thirty days hard labor or $100 fines. They chose jail, and eleven students were committed to a Southern road gang.

Other Negro prisoners held the student group in high esteem and asked them to settle arguments. Discussions of world problems began. The group conducted classes in English and current events. However, the students were not allowed to keep up with their studies. On the sixth day in jail the texts they had brought along were gathered up. "This is a prison—not a damned school," explained an officer.

Singing also got the demonstrators into trouble. The officials were tolerant in regard to the shouting and cursing of other prisoners, but when the demonstrators started morning devotions, the jailers objected to the songs used. They were particularly irked by the line: "Before I'll be a slave, I'll be buried in my grave."

The singers were told to stop. They didn't. An official claimed they were trying to run the prison. They came back with the argument that they were merely exercising their religious freedom. "If y'all are that religious," the officer asked, "why ain't y'all preachers?" It was explained that two of them were in fact studying for the ministry. But they were nevertheless put in solitary confinement— once, then again.

The first kneel-ins occurred at Rock Hill in connection with these jail-ins. Though the town has many churches, the worship of God had been on a strictly segregated basis. When Negro "kneel-inners" tried to attend worship in the community, two white churches barred them, three admitted them.

On Lincoln's Birthday of 1961, more than 1,000 persons participated in a pilgrimage to Rock Hill. A few white drivers speeded cars up and down the road in an attempt to intimidate. Guards took notes as visitors spoke with the jail-inners. But, at last, agreement was reached that the lunch counters would be integrated in the fall. And in the meantime the jail-ins had spread to both Lynchburg and Atlanta.

After hearing the Rock Hill story, writer Lillian Smith said that she "couldn't shake it off" for days. She said it should not have happened but it did happen, "because we are a confused people . . . because too many of us bow down to the idol of racism instead of searching for the meaning of God for man."[1]

During this same period CORE initiated the so-called Freedom Rides—dramatic demonstrations in which whites and Negroes travel together to protest laws segregating terminal waiting rooms in the South. In a modification of this technique, a busload of Protestant Episcopal priests, both white and Negro, began a Prayer Pilgrimage at New Orleans in September, 1961. They were led by the Rev. John B. Morris, executive director of the Episcopal Society for Cultural and Racial Unity, an unofficial body that has created considerable opposition in some parts of that church. Drawing national attention to this particular group was the presence among them of the son-in-law of New York Gov. Nelson A. Rockefeller, the thirty-five-year-old Rev. Robert L. Pierson.

On the second day of their trip fifteen of them—twelve whites and three Negroes—entered a bus station waiting room at Jackson, Mississippi. Police Capt. J. L. Ray, who had already handled some 300 Freedom Rider arrests there, promptly ordered them arrested.

"I admire the courage and dedication of these young people to the basic precepts on which this country was founded," said Gov. Rockefeller.

They were praised also by the Rt. Rev. Arthur Lichtenberger, then presiding bishop of the Protestant Episcopal Church. He declared they were "attempting to bear witness to their Christian convictions about racial matters and to make it evident to the whole country what the position of the Episcopal Church is."

But some fellow Episcopalians attacked them on both legal and moral grounds. Bishop Charles C. J. Carpenter of

[1] Adapted from *Jailed-In*, by Thomas Gaither. New York: League for Industrial Democracy, 1961.

Alabama "thoroughly disapproved" of their plan to come to his state and said he would not meet them. "If you do come here purposely to break the laws of the state of Alabama, you can expect no help from us," he wrote. Bishop Wilburn Campbell of West Virginia said he had "little sympathy for them" because of their "immoral" tactics.

The priests set up a portable altar in the jail and celebrated Mass. The three Negro ministers were in a separate cell, but the whites were permitted to take sacraments to them. Two days after their arrest, they were fined $200 and sentenced to four-month terms. After six days behind bars, thirteen of them posted $500 bonds and were released, and they went on to the sixtieth General Convention of their church in Detroit. The two others, who remained symbolically for all, gained release ten days later by posting bonds.

One of the early Freedom Rides was in the news again in 1964 because of segregationist tenacity. Nine Northern white and Negro clergymen, including two rabbis, went to Tallahassee, Florida, in 1961 to attempt desegregation of eating facilities. They were arrested, and appeals over three years failed. Though the civil rights law was enacted in the meantime, they were legalistically brought back to jail in the summer of 1964 to serve ninety days on the old charge. They were put to such tasks as stacking bricks and cutting grass—prisoners at labor because they had taken a moral stand now supported by federal law!

Whether such a "ride" and "pilgrimage" helps overcome segregation has been endlessly debated. But like the surf turning cliffs into sand, each succeeding wave of protest apparently works to erode the rocks of resistance to integration.

While the civil rights bill was being debated, President Johnson reported on the degree of desegregation in accommodations already achieved. He said that out of 566 Southern cities with more than 10,000 population, lunch counters had been integrated in 344. Theaters, restaurants and hotels had been desegregated in more than 250 of them. Two-thirds of this change, he said, had come in the sixties.

As a sweater is reversed when drawn over the head, the whole strategy has been altered by passage of the civil rights law of 1964.

Formerly the struggle for integration of public accommodations often had to be carried on in the face of both law and custom; now the weight of the law has come down on the side of those who oppose segregation of terminals and counters and hotels. Today it is the segregationist who is placed in the position of having to defy law to maintain his "ideals," and while moral sentiments are angrily voiced in his behalf, it is not easy to find high ethical grounds on which to support an appeal against democratic rights and Christian brotherhood. Law and idealism are now geared together for integration.

Exclusion of persons from restaurants, hotels and other public accommodations solely because of race has been illegal since the Fourth of July in 1964. There were a few flurries of opposition at first. Most widely publicized was the case of an Atlanta man who waved a pistol, backed up by friends brandishing ax handles, when Negroes tried to eat at his restaurant. In Kansas City, a thirteen-year old boy from Mississippi was refused a haircut at a shop in a hotel where CORE was having a national convention, but hours later he got it. Compliance with the law was widely announced, moreover, by many who had opposed it. Second thoughts were succinctly expressed by a Nashville barber:

"I worried myself sick about this before it became law, but now that we have it, I'm going to comply. I figure I'll have only two or three Negro customers a year. Most

Negroes can't afford a $1.50 haircut, and they'll keep going to their own shops, which are cheaper."

Such signs of compliance do not mean that the struggle for equal use of public facilities has been won. As opponents of the act had argued, prejudice cannot be overcome by law.

Still, law is a useful crowbar to loosen old bigotries. Law will help, however, only as dedicated citizens attack the many inequalities still remaining.

As we have heard one young CORE leader say, whites now take demonstrations without blinking, and more dramatic and unusual techniques must be found. For when there is not drama and showy conflict, the white community settles back somnolently to let the Negro suffer pain and indignity, away from the mainstream of national life. Fears of backlash brought a moratorium to civil rights action groups before the 1964 elections, but countless more protests of various kinds will be necessary if real integration is to come in public accommodations by—say, 1970.

3 · *Challenge of Power: Voting*

> If an American, because his skin is dark, cannot eat lunch in a restaurant open to the public, if he cannot send his children to the best public school available, if he cannot vote for the public officials to represent him . . . then who among us would be content to have the color of his skin changed and stand in his place?
> —John F. Kennedy

For a century after the Emancipation Proclamation, the white population had an opportunity to grant full citizenship to the Negro. The opportunity was muffed.

As the go-slow people argue, some evolutionary progress was made, at least in some sections of the country. But as the Negro matured, and as the memories of slavery dimmed and slipped away, he began to get some of the restless spirit of Patrick Henry. For the Negro of the 1960's Tom Paine became a much more acceptable hero than Uncle Tom.

"What would *you* do if you were denied the right to vote, or eat where you want, or live where you wish?" the white citizen can be asked pointedly. Like a Minute Man of 1776, he may say he'd reach for his musket. Responsible Negro leaders recognize that no minority could win, or keep won, a bloody civil war for equality.

So thoughtful Negroes have naturally turned to the power they have, or might develop, without the threat of violence. Many have embraced the nonviolent philosophy of Martin

Luther King, Jr., and practically all are emphasizing the importance of voting. If an individual cannot vote, his citizenship is a mockery. But to vote, the citizen—whatever his race or color—has to be interested and trained and registered and, as every good ward-heeler knows, taken around to the polls.

Marshalling a Negro vote, even in the North, is not so easy as it might appear to the uninitiated. Since, on the local level, the two major parties often try to win minority loyalties by handing out a minor job or two, without showing any real interest in minority problems, the Negro voter may feel that neither party offers him a genuine home. In Chicago, for example, where Negroes are a fourth of the population, Negroes booed Democratic Mayor Richard J. Daley, in 1963, but they do not appear to be enthusiastic about Republican candidates either. The Chicago Urban League in a 1964 study discovered that fewer than half the Negroes there voted, as compared with about two-thirds of the whites; it attributed this relative indifference to apathy and to a form of political protest.

Nevertheless, the "Negro vote" is important in getting much legislation approved. In some industrial states, Negro voters were powerful enough to have a decisive influence on their Congressional representatives when the civil rights bill was being considered.

Because a moral issue was involved, and because churches spoke politically with greater vigor than usual, they too were a factor in passage of the bill. Both proponents and opponents emphasized the importance of the church role. Hubert H. Humphrey, at that time a senator and floor manager for the bill, asserted flatly: "The most important force at work today on behalf of civil rights is the churches —Catholic, Protestant and Jewish." A leader of the Southern opponents, Georgia Democratic Senator Richard B. Russell, considered the clergy their most formidable opponent; he complained bitterly that "groups of ministers from all over the nation" were descending on the capitol "sanctimoniously moralizing over what is essentially a political question." The columnist Drew Pearson, in speaking around the nation, found church leaders "militant in working for human dignity" and concluded: "Civil rights has done more to unite the churches of America than any single issue in American history."

One of the historic dramas of the fight for passage was the Interreligious Convocation on Civil Rights called in Washington during the spring of 1964 at a time when the fight for passage seemed to be bogging down. Next morning newspapers around the country front-paged this news. The *New York Times* allotted the major position to an account by Ben A. Franklin which began:

WASHINGTON, April 28—American religious leaders demanded tonight that the Senate pass the civil rights bill—immediately and intact—as a matter of primary morality.

They invoked the name of God in urging enactment of the measure.

Their call was not only for prayer, however. There were undisguised political implications, and church spokesmen said that "not since Prohibition" had religion in this country "roused itself to political action for good or ill."

They said there was "no precedent" for the scale and unity of the "social action" program begun here tonight . . . .

Tomorrow, the Protestant denominations begin a daily A.M. prayer service at the Lutheran Church of the Reformation on Capitol Hill.

The service is planned as an assembly point for the hundreds of clergymen the National Council of Churches said would come to Washington in the next few weeks to "frankly lobby" for the civil rights bill . . . .

Priests, ministers, rabbis and laymen came from all over the East and as far as Des Moines to overflow a gymnasium that holds 3,800. Eighty percent were white. *Commonweal,* the Catholic lay magazine, called it "an exciting and inspiring event" and observed: "If ever there was a public issue on which all churches can speak clearly and with one voice, civil rights is that issue."

Rabbi Maurice Eisendrath, president of the Union of American Hebrew Congregations, caught the spirit of the event in these words:

In former years, the role of religious groups was that of passive spectators, bleating occasional platitudes about brotherhood. Today, religious leaders are in the front lines of the battle, unafraid of the smoke and din of controversy and determined to press forward until the filibuster is broken . . ."

When the prayer vigil ended two months later with passage of the bill, one leader expressed surprise at "our political muscle."[1]

Meantime, students at Union Theological Seminary had conceived the idea of a silent vigil in Washington. Joined by Catholic and Jewish seminarians on Sunday, April 19, they took shifts standing silently, twenty-four hours a day, near the Lincoln Memorial. There, where thousands of high-school students and tourists pass on a typical day, they demonstrated "to speak the conscience of every man." One day they were joined by the president of Union, Dr. John C. Bennett, and a leader from both the Jewish Theological Seminary and Georgetown University (Catholic). That same day, in a counter-protest, George Lincoln Rockwell, commander of the American Nazi party, stood nearby with two grim-faced young men and a sign that read:

"American Nazi Party Vigil on Behalf of the White Christian Majority Which Opposes Minority Tyranny."

[1] "The Voice of the Churches," by William V. Shannon, in *The Commonweal,* May 15, 1964, pp. 226-228.

Fortunately, the majority of Congressmen saw that th
conscience of America was aroused and passed the law
Symbolically, in Brooklyn, 300 whites and Negroes, mem
bers of a Roman Catholic and a Lutheran Church, assem
bled to give thanks in prayer and to read a "Litany fo
Racial Justice" they had composed. Christians in many lo
calities gave expression in various ways to their gratitud
for this milestone in justice. History will undoubtedly giv
a large share of the credit for passage of the legislation t
pressures from the churches as well as from Negro actio
groups.

The new law recognized the demands of Negroes fo
their just share of political power. The first of its seve
titles deals with voting rights.

Almost a century ago, the Fifteenth Amendment to th
Constitution forbade the states to deny the vote to anyon
on account of race. The new measure tried to validate tha
guarantee by facilitating registration.

During the struggle in the Senate, bipartisan supporter
charged with passage of Title I—Republican Senator Ken
neth B. Keating of New York and Democratic Senator Phili
A. Hart of Michigan—produced astounding evidence of th
need for reformation. One Negro in Louisiana had bee
rejected for registration because he made an error of on
day in giving his age in years, months and days—he forgo
one month had 31 days instead of 30! In 1956, a little mor
than 5 percent of adult Negroes in 100 Southern countie
had been registered; six years later, the figure was still onl
8.3 percent. In 14 Mississippi counties with a total voting
age Negro population of more than 100,000 not one Negr
was registered. Only 8 Negroes were registered in a Flo
rida county with 300 Negro school teachers!

In some parts of the South, however, Negroes in larg
numbers had been registering and voting even before th

law was passed. And as might be expected, local governments were more responsive to Negro needs when they had to take into account repercussions at the polls.

E. H. (Boss) Crump of Memphis, who died in 1954, used a bloc of several thousand Negro voters in that county to help maintain his benevolent dictatorship, and in recent years NAACP registration drives have pushed the total of Negro voters in that county up to one-third of the electorate. Jesse H. Turner, president of the NAACP branch, has said: "We haven't elected a Negro to office yet, but we can decide which white man gets in."

Macon County, Alabama, is another area where Negro voters are gaining influence. This is the county where Booker T. Washington founded the famous Tuskegee Institute in 1881. Negroes who outnumber the whites four to one began to demand the right to vote there a few years ago, and by 1964 the number of registered Negroes had passed the number of whites registered in the county. In own, there were 1,133 Negro voters, 1,029 white. If the Negroes voted as a bloc, they could control the local government bodies. However, they decided not to let race become the determining factor in their voting. No Negro ran against the white mayor in the summer of 1964 election, but seven Negroes were candidates for the council. Most of them received only token votes. But two, the Rev. K. L. Buford and Sociology Professor Stanley Smith, won and became the first Negro councilmen in the community since Reconstruction. In November, four Negroes were elected to Macon County offices in another historic breakthrough.

President Johnson's landslide resulted partly from an overwhelming Negro vote. *Time* reported: "In a Negro precinct of Richmond, the vote was up 200% from 1960, and it went for Johnson, 1,257 to 4. Negroes gave Johnson much of his margin in Florida, went 98% for him in a

Jacksonville precinct."[2] The *New York Times* studied hard-fought House and Senate races won by Democrats in 1964 and found "a massive Negro vote was the decisive or an important element in all of them," South as well as North.

The logic of events forces Negroes to push on with registration and voting drives. Use of political power is an inevitable development for any dissatisfied minority in a democratic society, as illustrated in some cities by the precinct strength of today's Irish Catholics. (Their rise is sometimes held up erroneously as a pattern for Negroes in sections where color makes a bigger difference than national origin.) "The Supreme Court decision ten years ago had the ultimate effect of taking this urgent problem [civil rights] out of the judicial and putting it in the realm of politics," Professor Louis H. Pollack, a Yale University professor of constitutional law, said recently. "They put it up to communities like yours and mine."

During the sixties, therefore, the objective of one of the major waves of civil rights agitation was to secure votes for Negroes in Southern states. Some Northerners, both Negroes and whites, took part in this drive, so the plaint was often voiced that "outside agitators" were disturbing peaceful communities. Two decades before, young Negro men, both North and South, had been called by the draft to become "outside agitators" to correct injustice overseas. But that was thousands of miles away, and to the voting registrar or peace justice in many a hamlet, it was quite different from "interference" here at home.

One dramatic story came out of Terrell County in western Georgia in the summer of 1962. Negroes ran into resistance and intimidation when they wanted to register. A federal judge had ordered that their voting rights be recognized.

[2] *Time,* November 4, 1964, p. 4.

But as 70-year-old Sheriff Zeke Mathews explained to *New York Times* reporter, Claude Sitton, the whites were "a little fed up with this registration business." They knew that the Negroes, outnumbering whites almost two to one, could overwhelm them at the polls if democracy were instituted. Of the 4,533 whites in the county, 2,894 were registered; but of the approximately 9,000 Negroes, there were only 51 Negro voters on the rolls.

"We want our colored people to go on living like they have for the last hundred years," the sheriff explained blandly.

But members of the Student Nonviolent Coordinating Committee (Snick) moved in and called a voter registration meeting at a Baptist church in Sasser. The sheriff arrived to say he was concerned because "disturbed white citizens" were gathering outside. Inside, there were, in addition to three reporters, thirty-eight Negroes and two white students—22-year-old Ralph Allen from Massachusetts and 18-year-old Penelope Patch of Swarthmore College.

Charles Sherrod, a 25-year-old Negro from Virginia, led in the Lord's Prayer after the opening hymn. He read from the Scriptures. Then he read the passage again because the "disturbed" citizens were still there.

Gnats circled three light bulbs above. In the July night outside there were crickets, but angry voices rose above them. Someone was yelling out the numbers of license plates.

Then suddenly thirteen law officers and roughly-dressed whites clumped in. Mr. Sherrod prayed: "Oh, Lord God, we've been abused so long; we've been down so long; oh, Lord, all we want is for our white brothers to understand that in thy sight we are all equal . . ."

The congregation swung into "We Are Climbing Jacob's Ladder." Then Zeke Mathews strode down front and announced that though he respected religion, "My people is getting disturbed about these secret meetings."

Informing the reporters that none of the local Negroes was dissatisfied, he asked the Negroes to stand. "Are any of you disturbed?"

"Yes," came the muffled reply.

"Do you need people to come down and tell you what to do?"

"Yes."

Unabashed, the sheriff declared, "There's not a nigger in Terrell County who needs someone from elsewhere to help him vote."

Then a deputy, who had been fingering a hand-tooled black leather cartridge belt and a .38 revolver, took the floor. Though year-round registration is provided by Georgia law, he issued the fiat: "There is a prohibit to register between now and December." Five months!

Deputies started taking down the names of local Negroes. Referring to Allen, one of them said, "He's going to be gone in two weeks, but you'll still be here."

The Negroes began humming the protest song, "We shall Overcome," and as the officers left, it swelled to a crescendo like a mighty hymn.[3]

Civil rights law or no law, it is obvious that in such areas Negroes in large numbers are no more likely to be voting soon than in South Africa. But by some bizarre logic, if someone in Washington should try to help those potential voters get their constitutional rights, many people would think of him not as a Lincoln but a Hitler!

During August, 1963, CORE conducted a drive in Iberville Parish, Louisiana, to obtain voting privileges and other opportunities for Negroes who had been gerrymandered out of Plaquemine, the parish's largest town. James

[3] The story was recounted in the *New York Times,* July 27, 1962.

Farmer, national CORE leader, with three local men, led 500 persons on a protest march to City Hall. The leaders were arrested, and the others were dispersed by a teargas attack. Mr. Farmer remained in jail for ten days and as a result missed the March on Washington.

"The historic March on Washington would go on beautifully without us," Mr. Farmer recalls. "The historic struggle of Plaquemine Negroes might not. The magnificent demonstration in Washington inspired Plaquemine's freedom fighters to redouble their efforts. They marched and they sat-in. They were tear gassed, struck with electric prod rods and trampled by state troopers' horses."

With the leaders out of jail, the largest demonstration of all began in September. Mr. Farmer dramatically describes what followed:

Mounted troopers with their prod rods, rode down the marchers like cowboys on a fearsome round-up. The demonstrators again took refuge in Freedom Rock Baptist Church. Troopers pursued them into the church, hurling round after round of tear gas canisters. The demonstrators were driven from the church, carrying the wounded, the faint and the hysterical. They retreated to the parsonage.

Not content with this desecration of a place of worship, the troopers turned high-pressure fire hoses into the church, overturning benches and breaking windows. Bibles and hymnals floated in the pews.

The Negroes turned to a boycott. A worker in a Negro school lunchroom was fired because her children had demonstrated, and the students boycotted the lunchroom, singing freedom songs instead of eating. In October, Negro students struck and forced closing of the high school. They assembled once more in the church, and again police teargassed them.

"It was on this occasion," writes Mr. Farmer, "that Police Chief Dennis Songy threatened to destroy the church, asserting: If they want to use that church to serve God, that's OK, but they're not going to use it as a fort."[4] Although the protest was peaceful, the chief apparently believed it was for him to decide how Americans could use their church.

Only a week later the Rev. Joseph Carter became the first Negro to register in sixty-two years in one of the parishes of this Congressional district. In a second parish a full slate of twelve Negroes ran for office in the Democratic primary.

Change was taking place, but it was so slow, sporadic and scattered that the rights organizations planned still bigger drives. In late February, 1964, a group of 350 Negroes lined up for five hours in the chill to register at Canton, Mississippi. Many arrived from the environs on foot or in mulecarts. This was the biggest voter demonstration test so far in the state, but CORE reported that only five were admitted to take the registration test. Then the Southern Christian Leadership Conference, headed by Dr. Martin Luther King, also started to train people to push registration. The Rev. Andrew Young, executive director of the conference, said it would take 270 years to register Mississippi's Negroes if the process weren't speeded up.

Meantime white reaction started. The old Ku Klux Klan burgeoned. The Americans for the Preservation of the White Race was founded in 1963, and at a Mississippi court house meeting, one leader, Arsene Dick, an electrician, asserted that there were 30,000 to 40,000 members in Mississippi and Louisiana. Though he claimed the movement was nonviolent, he told *New York Times* reporter Sitton: "A man today who hasn't got a gun in his house is a fool."

[4] This story was recounted in *Louisiana Story, 1963,* by James Farmer. New York: CORE, 1963.

A mechanic nearby allegedly put in: "We ought to get shed of all of 'em. We ought to shoot 'em all."

This attitude was being carried out in Mississippi through terrorism, intimidation and murder. In 1961, Herbert Lee, a Negro farmer active in voter registration, had been killed by a state representative in what was ruled justifiable homicide. In January, 1964, one of the few witnesses of that shooting, Louis Allen, a Negro logger, was murdered. Four other Negroes were killed in the same section in half a year, others flogged. Homes were fired into. On one night in April, crosses were burned in sixty-four of Mississippi's eighty-two counties.

E. W. Steptoe, Sr., president of the NAACP in one county, said he couldn't understand why the whites were so bitter about Negro desires. "They're not asking for nothing out of reason—just the vote." Despite a three year registration drive, he said his son was the only registered Negro voter in the county.

Churches that were alive inevitably got into this struggle of citizenship. In an interview during a recent Northern speaking tour, John Lewis, the national chairman of Snick, explained that much of the voter organizing was done in the churches, especially in Mississippi, because the church is a major means of communication. Mr. Lewis, chairman for two years of the Nashville Student Movement, had been graduated from American Baptist Seminary and was studying at Fisk.

The ministers were cooperative, he explained, and announcements to the Negro community could readily be made at 11 A.M. services in the South.

"Do the ministers lead, or do the people push them to be more active?" a CORE leader asked.

"The people push them," he said.

Mr. Lewis explained that the Southern Negro minister

tended to be conservative. That does not necessarily mean he is an "Uncle Tom" playing ball with the white power structure—he is just trying to avoid controversy and get along. However, Mr. Lewis went on to say that the role of the church is vital, and the race movement is helping it strengthen.

"Young people," he said, "are getting more interested in the church because of it."

In the spring of 1964, the Commission on Religion and Race of the National Council of Churches noted "unparalleled student concern" in regard to Negro voting. The Council of Federated Organizations (COFO), guided by Snick and made up of rights groups, was planning an all-out voter registration drive in the Deep South, using student registrars. The staff of the commission felt that it would be foolish, and perhaps dangerous, for scores of college youth to rush into areas of unfamiliar social climate without screening and without training. They therefore undertook to cooperate with COFO by providing minister-counselors for the students and by helping with a course of orientation training.

Up to a thousand students went into the Deep South in the voter registration drive. In June, the first wave of 200 took an orientation course at a college in Oxford, Ohio.

A Mississippi newspaper called the ecumenical action "incredibly criminal." The Louis Harris Poll found American public opinion opposed to the student's going by a two to one margin. When Southern Presbyterians protested the council's use of "immature persons," General Secretary R. H. Edwin Espy wired that the National Council had not recruited students but had sent ministers and lawyers as counselors and had helped with orientation "to prepare them spiritually for this very demanding experience."

The students were given a handbook that urged them not

to stand in lighted doorways or to travel at night. Whether they would be jailed was relatively unimportant, said James Forman, a Snick leader, adding: "I may be killed and you may be killed."

The words proved prophetic. Five days later, on a Sunday, three of the young registration workers disappeared. James E. Chaney, a 21-year-old Mississippi Negro, and Michael H. Schwerner, a 24-year-old white New Yorker, were both rights workers, and the third, Andrew Goodman, white and 20, was a volunteer fresh from the Oxford course. Their burned station wagon was found, and America followed the search for the young men or their bodies on television. FBI agents massed. J. Edgar Hoover himself went in. There was talk of a hoax.

Back at Oxford, the word came to the next wave of trainees. "We should dedicate ourselves in their names," said one leader. No one dropped out of the course, and at the end of the week a second wave of 300 went into Mississippi.

At last, six weeks after the three workers had disappeared, their bodies were unearthed from a secluded dam. A New York doctor said that the bones of one, the Negro, were as badly shattered as if he had been in a plane crash.

Thousands crowded a memorial service for the trio in New York, attended by their parents. At its end, the three mothers—two white and one Negro—linked arms as they walked out.

The Rev. Dr. Dan Potter, executive director of the city's Protestant Council, suggested that the men be buried in Arlington Cemetery: "These young men gave their lives in the cause of liberty as truly and heroically as any American ever has in war or peace."

In a press conference called for the Goodman parents, Mrs. Goodman said: "The values our son expressed in his single action of going to Mississippi are still the bonds that bind this nation together . . . . We shall continue to work for this goal."

Was the sacrifice meaningful?

In Mississippi, terror continued. All summer, night riders used guns, dynamite, tear gas and Molotov cocktails to harrass the rights workers and Negroes. Nightsticks flailed and over 100 pickets were arrested during a demonstration as scores of Negroes waited to register at one courthouse. Churches were burned. COFO said fifty-two men were beaten. Rabbi Arthur J. Lelyveld of Cleveland and two young white rights workers were battered with a heavy iron bar. The Rev. Edward K. Heininger, minister of an interdenominational fellowship at Drake University in Iowa, reported he was beaten in a Mississippi doctor's office to which he had taken a Harvard student. In another town, rights workers were sprayed with household deodorant, and the Rev. Tom Pendleton, a white minister from Waterbury, Connecticut, said he was ordered out of town by police. A few days before the election in the fall of 1964, a group including seven out-of-state ministers was arrested at Magnolia after they had made repeated attempts to stage a voter drive.

Drew Pearson devoted a column to describing the hate campaign directed at a native Mississippian. Albert W. Heffner, a white insurance man in McComb and father of Miss Mississippi for 1964, said he hadn't even believed in integration. But through his pastor he met Don McCord, a rights worker of the National Council of Churches, and extended an invitation to dinner. The upshot was that hundreds made harassing phone calls, and Mr. Heffner's business dropped to zero. The family had to leave the town and state.

In spite of harassments, however, forty-seven "freedom

schools" were held, and a few hundred managed to register to vote in Mississippi.

The National Council of Churches, in the meantime, had recognized that an on-going, deep-rooted operation was needed to follow up the voter registration drive, and the Delta Ministry was established. A quarter-million dollar program in Mississippi was initiated in September, 1964, to deal with persistent poverty and racial injustice. As a result, the United States became a kind of "mission area," for the World Council of Churches undertook to supply 40 percent of the cost.

"Sister churches in other areas should be involved in meeting this great need," explained the Rev. W. A. Visser 't Hooft, Dutch general secretary, "and they [American churches] wish to profit by the experience of other Christians who have ministered in areas of great tension . . . The Mississippi Delta is a symbol of resistance to full racial equality, and the race problem is a world problem which the whole Christian world must help to solve."

The Delta Ministry includes programs in health, relief, literacy, community center work, and citizenship education. It is based on the recognition that, along with voting rights, many doors to opportunity need to be opened simultaneously.

More than two million Negroes in eleven Southern states can now vote. In the decade 1952-62, about 350,000 registered; half a million have registered since. The national total is now about six million. But three million eligible Southern Negroes remain unregistered as the drive continues.

Two-thirds of the eligible Negroes are registered in Tennessee, which leads the eleven states. Mississippi is at the bottom, with 6.7 percent. Negroes in that state have organized well enough, however, to launch a Mississippi

Freedom Party, as everyone knows who watched the 1964 Atlantic City Convention on TV. This integrated organization is fighting to replace the state's regular segregated Democratic party, which worked for the right-wing Republicans on the national level. Democrats nationally are being forced to confront this problem, and will have to resolve it before the 1968 election.

Georgia suggests the kind of change that can be hoped for in the Deep South. About two out of five eligible Negroes there are registered. Student volunteers have worked in Georgia too, and in one rural county the number of registered Negroes was increased during the summer of 1964 from 300 to 1,350 (out of a possible 6,500). In Albany, 500 were registered. For the first time in almost a century, a Negro ran for Congress in southwest Georgia. Atlanta elected its first Negro, B. L. Dent, to its City Council. And also for the first time two Negro delegates and two Negro alternates were named to the state's Democratic delegation of the 1964 convention.

"This is a political organization," explained Gov. Carl E. Sanders as he named the Negroes, "and it is right and proper that we have a cross section of the voters of the state represented."

Which is certainly a fresh new note from the South!

PART THREE

CIRCLE OF FRUSTRATION

4 · The Interlocked Demands

> It is evident that in large part Negroes are so poor because they are so badly educated and they are so badly educated because their parents are so poor.
> —Walter Lippmann

What does the Negro want?

"We want jobs, housing and quality integrated education —and we want them *now*," James Farmer of CORE, replied to Gertrude Samuels, an interviewer for the *New York Times Magazine*.

"We are concerned with jobs, education, housing," Roy Wilkins, executive secretary of the NAACP, ticked off for her.

These statements from leaders were confirmed by popular polls. *Newsweek* and the Louis Harris polling organization, in a cooperative study reported in 1963, found that nationwide, 64 percent of Negroes want integrated housing. Seven out of ten Negroes desire mixed schools. The Negro "wants a better job, better pay, a better home," *Newsweek* summarized.[1]

More recently, the Kraft polling organization and the *New York Times* conducted a survey of New York Negroes.

[1] See *Newsweek*, July 29, 1963, pp. 15f, and October 21, 1963, pp. 44f.

"Most list unemployment, poor housing, poor schools and high rents as the most pressing problems in their neighborhoods," the *New York Times* reported. To these traditional complaints they added their fear of muggers, hoods, dope addicts and "winos" who prey on their own race in the slum areas. Here are the figures (with some people listing more than one answer) for the question: "What would you say is the biggest problem that Negroes here in this part of the city have to worry about?":

Economics (jobs, living cost, etc.)	54%
Housing (bad, overcrowded, high rents, etc.)	49
Crime and criminals	39
Education	32

What kind of schools did they want? "Just a good school," said one out of four. But two-thirds specified an integrated one, and only one in twenty-five of those interviewed wanted an all-Negro school.

But don't Negroes prefer to live among Negroes? Only 10 percent indicated a preference for an all-Negro neighborhood; 44 percent wanted an integrated one, and the rest didn't have a preference.

In a recent month in New York State, these poll figures were given concrete reality by the report of the state Commission on Human Rights. There were only six complaints about public accommodations, but there were fifty-six allegations of job discrimination. The highest number of complaints—fifty-eight—were related to housing discrimination. A survey of a small Connecticut city with seventy-seven Negro families showed that high rents and lack of good housing were their major concerns.

While the battles are not won for those objectives discussed in earlier chapters—access to accommodations and voting rights—the struggle has moved onto these other fronts in much of the nation. In large resisting pockets of the South, equal treatment at lunch counters and in parks and at the polls must still be battled for. But in most of the North, the revolution centers now around three demands: jobs, houses, schools.

The Negro wants a decent home. To afford it, he needs a good job. To obtain that, he needs an education. To get an education for a dignified place in a pluralistic society, he has to go to a good, integrated school—and that means a good home in an integrated neighborhood—and a good job— so the circle goes round. And in reverse, the circle spins viciously—poor housing, weak education, menial jobs. Then frustration and hate and perhaps violence.

The figures in the *Newsweek* poll indicate where the clashes of Negro and white attitudes come and why the irresistible force appears to be meeting the immovable object. Fewer than half the white people polled would object to having a child bring a Negro youngster home for a meal, or to their children going to an integrated school, or to sitting next to a Negro on a bus, in a movie or at a lunch counter. Moreover, in both North and South well over 90 percent approve of the Negro's having the right to vote.

So far, the attitudes seem hopeful.

What, specifically, of jobs, housing and schools? Here again the figures seem hopeful at first glance. Among the whites, nation-wide, 80 percent said they favored better job opportunities for Negroes, 85 percent good housing and 75 percent integrated schools (in the South the percentage ranged from 81 to 43 on these subjects).

The poll indicated the outlook was best for jobs. *Newsweek* said that most Negroes and whites agree that Negro jobs are not equal now, that job integration is OK, and that employment will improve for Negroes in coming years.

Even in the South, fewer than half the whites said they would object to working next to a Negro.

But in housing, the strong tally for "good housing" was not necessarily for good mixed housing. More than half the whites want no federal law on housing. Only 42 percent want integrated housing.[2] And slightly more than half prefer not to have a Negro living next door.

In short, the typical white man talks as if he is for equality but, in such areas as housing, he often doesn't want equality to mean integration. As a seventy-year-old Negro woman, a pensioner in Chicago, put it: "The white man is all mix up. He'd like to do better, but he's all mix up."

In the next chapters, we shall take a closer look at the problems and progress in the fields where Negroes most want change—and then at the danger of violence when change does not come fast enough.

[2] Polls summarized recently in the *Scientific American* showed that in two decades the percentage of Southern whites approving integrated schools has risen from 2 to 30. Their acceptance of residential integration rose meantime from 12 to 51 percent; among Northerners, this change was from 42 to 70; both recent figures are notably higher than the *Newsweek* figures. A later poll of white New Yorkers reported by the *New York Times* said 57 percent would not be uncomfortable having one or two Negro families living near; 40 percent said they would be uncomfortable with "a number" of such families—but 15 percent said they wouldn't be troubled if they were the only whites in a block.

5 · Struggle for Good Homes

I would ask you to involve yourselves. The crisis in communities North and South in such matters as housing, employment, public accommodations and schools is steadily mounting. It is the duty of every Christian citizen to know fully what is happening in his own community, and actively support efforts to meet the problems he encounters.
—Arthur Lichtenberger, formerly presiding bishop of Protestant Episcopal Church

In the Mohawk Valley industrial city of Utica, in upstate New York, the city hired a new director of human relations. He was a Negro, Paul Richardson.

White friends offered to help him find a place to live, but he wanted to get an apartment on his own, simply as a Negro citizen. When he looked, he did not identify himself by job or mention his college master's degree.

Mr. Richardson searched for a week, applying at a dozen places. One owner advertised an apartment for $50, but when Mr. Richardson got there it was $65. At another place where he applied in person he was quoted a price of $85, but when he telephoned the next day without indicating that he was a Negro, he was told the price was "under $75."

At another door, he rapped and heard a dog bark inside. He could see people through the glass. But no answer.

Finally he gave up and took an apartment in a predominantly Negro section.

"I ghettoed myself in," he said simply.

So have most American Negroes, and not voluntarily.

White opposition has been expressed to housing integration, sometimes frighteningly, throughout the North as well as in the South.

Over church and synagogue opposition, voters in Detroit in 1964 adopted a "homeowners rights ordinance" that sought to legalize housing segregation. Voters approved similar measures in Tacoma, Washington; Akron, Ohio; and Berkeley, California. A major issue of the November election in California was Proposition 14. Catholics, Protestants and Jews opposed this housing discrimination law, and the *Economist* of London reported "the best hope for defeating it seems to lie in the churches"—but it passed, by more than two to one.

In Seattle, voters rejected two to one a proposal to ban racial or religious discrimination in the sale or rent of property. The Rev. Dr. John H. Adams, pastor of the First African Methodist Episcopal Church, said it showed that "two thirds of the people of Seattle, in essence, don't want the Negro living next door to them." In the University of Washington section of the city, a Presbyterian minister, the Rev. Dr. Robert Boyd Munger, distributed cards at Sunday services for the signature by "a Christian citizen" of pledges not to discriminate in selling or renting. Only 75 of the 2,200 who attended that day signed cards.

In spite of sporadic white resistance, however, there has been a steady flow of Negroes into some good neighborhoods. In a Teaneck, New Jersey, area of $20,000 homes, there are more than 400 Negroes among the 8,000 population. Says a newspaper account: "White and Negro children play together, the parents of both belong to the Parent-

Teacher Association and attend the same churches. There is very little social intercourse, however."

In the new suburb of Canoga Park, north of Los Angeles, the Bob Maxwells—Negroes—bought a house. Phones buzzed. A real estate agent, scenting a financial killing, called people in the neighborhood with "inside advice"— urging them to sell before what he claimed would be an inevitable drop in property values. Some panicked and put signs up. Bob Barnes of the AP tells the rest of the story:

> Into the melee of human emotions stepped a young Methodist minister and several associates. They went from door to door, spreading facts, soothing fears.
>
> That was five years ago. Now the Maxwells attend theater parties in mixed groups, entertain Caucasians and Negroes alike at New Year's Eve shindigs, belong to a white Protestant church—but keep up their old associations as well.
>
> Houses across the street and two doors each way have sold, in the normal course of events and at the market price, to new white people.[1]

But the idea dies hard that property values will decline if Negroes move in. The fact that the high demand by Negroes and the short supply of housing for them must surely push prices up is ignored even by economic conservatives. It is also overlooked that the Negro who wants to buy a better home and can afford to is probably an outstanding person who has had something of an Horatio Alger success against great odds.

Panic started at Negro moves in Baltimore, Maryland, but the city used its reason and formed Baltimore Neighborhoods, Inc. The goal of white homeowning members is to stabilize neighborhoods where change is occurring, and the staff has had some success in easing integration problems. While most Negroes are still concentrated in an old area, there are some in all but seven of 168 census districts, and a

[1] *The New York Times,* December 23, 1962.

dozen Negro families have even moved into "exclusive" Northwood without mishap. When there is no panic, prices steady.

Of course, a major cause for fear of Negro neighbors is that most whites know few Negroes, and so stereotypes persist. For example, the Negro is said to be dirty.

Dr. Warren C. Haggstrom, social work professor at Syracuse University, answers this misconception with facts: "I studied the relative cleanliness of interiors of Negro and white dwellings in a sample of comparable households in low income neighborhoods in a city in the northern United States. Of twenty dwellings with Negro occupants, eighteen were kept reasonably clean. However, of thirty white households of the same economic level, only fifteen were kept reasonably clean. In other words, half the white households in the sample failed to meet this standard, but only 10 percent of the Negro households fell below it. Yet the prevalent view of that city is that Negroes are not good housekeepers."

Then this white professor adds the clincher: "The fact that Negro women from low income areas not only do their own housework but also are largely responsible for the cleanliness of houses in prosperous sections of the white community is conveniently ignored."

Real estate men must take much of the responsibility for continuing the myths about integrated housing. Often they seek refuge in the excuse that they are simply businessmen representing prejudiced owners, but the persistence of realtors' conservatism suggests that a good deal of the bigotry is in the salesmen themselves.

Are the two writers of this book being starry-eyed dreamers about integrated housing? No, we live in a section of a Northern city which in 1950 had virtually no Negroes except a maid or two, but today there are scattered Negro families throughout our neighborhood. We also have a Catholic school and convent, Jews and some Oriental students: pluralistic America! As integration came, some whites protested. Only one or two real estate men have been much positive help to Negroes, but all keep selling to whites. Property values are steady. You can't tell a Negro house from a white one by walking down the streets. And you'll see white children playing happily with an occasional Negro child and all of them going off to the same neighborhood school (now somewhat integrated, with a minimum of bussing and fussing).

If white owners will substitute realism and charity for myths and stereotypes, Negro families can live next door happily.

There have been two major pressures toward integration of housing.

First, the Negro family with middle-class income and aspirations wants a middle-class home, not a slum shack. To put it most simply, he wants to be able to move anywhere he can afford. If he wants a shady little place on the edge of town, he wants to be free to buy it. If he wants to be on the fifth floor of a new garden-type apartment or a split-level in a new suburban development, he wants to be free to get that. This is a right that the most disreputable white takes completely for granted. Like the white, the Negro wants "a better place" as his income goes up and, inevitably, that means a place in a "white neighborhood" near a "white school."

The other big factor pushing the Negro out of old homes is the nationwide drive of urban renewal—or as some call it bitterly, "Negro removal." The blighted sections near city business districts had to go—but these are the neighborhoods in which countless Northern Negro families have lived. New business buildings and civic centers have been put in, fine

for the eye of white travelers but of little use to the dis-
placed Negroes. Sleek apartments have arisen, but often at
rentals prohibitive to these Negroes. Downtown real estate
has revived, to the profit of big owners—but often the
human needs of Negroes and Puerto Ricans have been forgotten, or, at best, casually treated. They have had to press
out into dilapidated fringe areas, which have tended to
convert into overcrowded new slums, sometimes as segregated as the old. Civil rights groups, trying to find a handle
to deal with this evil, have protested and demonstrated
and often been misunderstood. Sometimes the conscience
of the church has made it cry out that as much consideration
should be given to the relocation of Negroes as is given to
the relocation of Central European D.P.'s or Hungarian
refugees.

*Finding a place to live is traumatic for me. I telephone in
answer to an ad, ask the landlord the usual questions—what
rent is being asked? Are the stove and refrigerator included
in the rental? The conversation moves into more treacherous
waters. The landlord begins to ask questions: Where do you
work? Where do you live now?*

*I wonder whether to fence, giving vague answers, not
letting him know just yet that I am a Negro. Perhaps, pray
God, this is a landlord who doesn't care. We finally agree
on a time when I can see the house. I am torn as to whether
to blurt out as we are about to ring off, "By the way, do you
have any objections to Negroes?" But I decide to wait until
he sees me.*

*The hours between the phone call and the interview leave
me in a cold sweat. The landlord wasn't too fussy about
children, but it is a downstairs flat, he has said, and two old
ladies live upstairs. When I go there and he discovers I am
Negro, will he use this as an excuse?*

The majority of churchmen have been apathetic. But in countless ways a minority of them have helped ease the housing integration crisis, as individuals and as groups, often unsung. St. Matthew's Episcopal Church of Evanston, Illinois, took a newspaper display ad to affirm support of equality and extend an invitation to persons of all races and creeds to worship there. The Catholic International Council of Chicago honored four clergymen—a Catholic priest, a Methodist minister, and two rabbis—who had given suburban Skokie "outstanding leadership" during the crisis that arose when its first Negro family moved there in 1961.

Obviously the church has not been the only institution aiding with Negro relocation. But here are three illustrations of cooperative church activity, a listing intended not to be exhaustive but suggestive:

New Haven—A rundown Negro area near Yale University in the heart of this Connecticut city is being transformed into an interracial neighborhood. A quarter of the area was demolished and the rest renovated, as $20 million of private, city and federal funds were pumped in.

Neighborhood churches played an important role in the overall planning. They also sponsored construction of 200 cooperative housing units. The Dixwell Congregational Church sponsored a $1.75 million apartment house with 129 units. A Roman Catholic parish, with an integrated congregation and school, sponsored 50 units.

New York City—"Each One Find One" is the slogan of a program started in cooperation with the city's Department of Relocation. Six religious groups representing the three major faiths united to try to find apartments for Negro and other families uprooted by public projects.

Priests, rabbis and ministers sent out a letter asking each

congregation to find "at least one good standard apartment
and list it with the city.

"Where necessary, the city will delay or postpone reloca
tion of families until we can find adequate housing fo
them," the clergymen wrote. "The city has a heart. May w
ask you to open your heart and join the city in carrying ou
our community responsibility?"

Meantime, New York City had been the demonstratio
area of a project for the National Committee Against Dis
crimination in Housing, a federation of thirty-nine nationa
organizations.

Noting that movement of Negroes and Puerto Ricans ou
of the ghettoes was very slow, the committee found that on
reason was lack of knowledge on the part of ghetto familie
as to how to find accommodations in distant white areas. S
a map was made showing white areas where there was
fairly constant vacancy rate in modest housing. Then th
committee worked through labor, religious and civic group
to find residents in these areas who were willing to be th
nucleus of a fair housing group. These volunteers collecte
information on such things as schools and transportation
and this was fed through professional groups and socia
clubs to the minority groups.

In the first six months of the project, community profile
were developed on fourteen neighborhoods. Twenty-fiv
families moved as a result, some of them to Long Island.

Syracuse—Two men, a Catholic and a Protestant, wer
behind a "church sponsorship" program which got nationa
attention. One of them was William M. Chiles, a Catholi
layman and a Negro, soft spoken but sometimes outspoken
The other was the Rev. Leon D. Sanborne, pastor of th
Robinson Memorial United Presbyterian Church in one o
the city's overwhelmingly white western suburbs.

In the fifties, Negro movements into white areas had been slow. The Quakers had brought a young white man, Bob Hale, into the community to work on housing integration, and he had been taken over as relocation director by the city. When Mr. Hale moved to a higher job, Mr. Chiles succeeded him.[2] During 1961, the new city relocation director made thirty-one talks to various groups, including a large number of church organizations. He pleaded for help in relocating some 900 families—mostly Negro—from slums that were to be demolished. It was only after the thirtieth talk, Mr. Chiles recalls, that he received from Mr. Sanborne the first offer of help.

The Board of Deacons of Robinson Memorial had held a series of meetings on inner-city life. In one of these meetings Mr. Chiles had suggested that a church "adopt" or sponsor a family whose home was to be torn down for urban renewal; a few individuals could meet the family, learn their problems and needs, and work with them to find a place.

Mr. Sanborne and four members volunteered. In January, Mr. Chiles phoned them about a family that he felt would welcome help.

"It was a young couple with four children under 4 years of age," Mr. Sanborne recalls. "To pay the exorbitant rent of $125 a month for four small, dark, dingy rooms, heated only by the kitchen oven, the father worked 15 hours a day, 7 to 10, six days a week on one job, and from 10 P.M. to 2 A.M. in another job.

"Instead of buying a car or T.V. set, he was buying furniture for a decent home into which he hoped he might move. Hard worker, dependable, nice, sufficient income—

[2] For the complete story, see "A Typical City—Case Study," Ch. 8, in *Progress Against Prejudice*, by Robert Root. New York: Friendship Press, 1957.

the only thing that prevented his having a decent home was the color of his skin.

"All we would do was to offer them our friendship in a genuine way, and try to help them find a home for themselves and those four sweet children. They were willing to move anywhere, they told us, that a landlord was willing to rent to them. But where?"

After meeting the family, the volunteers were so enthusiastic they started a "windshield survey" immediately–checking "For Rent" signs as they drove around in a car. The first two places spotted were too small. The owners of the third had to be tracked down by phone.

"When we did find them," Mr. Sanborne recounts, "they were ready to rent—until we told them the family was Negro. Oh, they were willing and would like to, they said, but the house had just been sold and they would have to ask the new owner. A few days later they called. 'Sorry but no.'"

The group found another place. Again the owners said they would think it over. Two days later they gave their answer: "No." Mr. Sanborne thought of Christ's words of judgment: "I was a stranger and you did not welcome me."

The group now found an ad listing "no discrimination." But on investigation they learned that the city had condemned the place. They found another that would welcome Negroes—but it had faulty wiring, narrow stairways, it was a "fire-trap, actually, and also condemned."

Mr. Sanborne and his group followed up seventy leads and made fifty visits—not until then did they find a suitable place. That same day the family found one on its own. So the house the church had discovered was offered to another family on Mr. Chiles' list.

The Robinson Memorial story aroused interest. Mr. Sanborne spoke to various churches and to a group of

Protestant, Catholic and Jewish leaders. Within two years, thirty-nine churches had joined in the sponsorship program. One or two of them relocated half a dozen families apiece. Others took pride in having found places for "impossible" families, a mother on welfare with ten children, in one instance; a mother with eight children in another. The priest of St. Therese' Catholic Church tells with good humor how laymen of his parish found an apartment for its assigned family and then joined the father, a devout and somewhat wary Baptist, in painting it.

Looking back, Mr. Chiles recalls that the tremendous job of sponsorship was tackled by churchmen with no expert knowledge.

"Nearly all the participants were people of extremely limited experience in the field of race relations," he says.

In the middle of 1964 the relocation office announced that, except for a few hard-core cases, the uprooted 900 families had all moved to new homes. The churches had helped the office with about 100 families but had probably not done the major share of the relocation for more than two or three dozen.

One thing that had not been accomplished to any impressive degree was indicated by Mr. Chiles' office map. It showed that there were still only a few dozen Negro families scattered through the city in nonsegregated neighborhoods, and that there were new concentrations in near-ghettoes close to the old ones. Mr. Chiles concludes that no great change in housing patterns has yet been brought about.

In the talks that he still makes to church groups (he's given over 130), Mr. Chiles emphasizes that one of the major values of the program has been educating white citizens about the enormity of the housing segregation problem. He sums up the positive aspects:

"Many of the ministers and priests are now able to preach on the topic of racial discrimination in housing from personal knowledge and experience. . . . It was also a new experience for most of the lay folk. . . . Meeting and getting acquainted with Negro families, and visiting them in their homes, was for nearly all of the sponsorship groups a new and rewarding experience."

Why don't churches and church people buy or build to sell or rent to Negroes? Why not back up convictions with cash?

A challenge to such action is provided by George Wilson of Newark, Delaware. He is not a wealthy white man but a builder and a Negro—the first Negro elected to the Newark City Council (his family was the first Negro one in First Presbyterian Church there).

In a *Presbyterian Life* interview, Mr. Wilson explained that he was building homes in two small integrated developments, not for profit but to provide "good houses for people who have been condemned by color, not by choice, to live in slum housing."

"I've seen too much hate," he said. "I've been hated too much myself. I'm not trying to act like Jesus Christ when I say this. I have a feeling that Christianity is something like not hating, doing things that really count. . . ."

The lesson learned by another Negro businessman is useful in thinking about the struggle for decency in housing.

John H. Johnson, the Negro publisher, founded the *Life*-like magazine for Negroes, *Ebony*, at a time when not many Negroes owned homes. They moved a lot. Few had checking accounts. In the years after World War II, *Ebony* boomed, using a sensational formula. But then in the fifties, circulation dropped off. Mr. Johnson looked around. He found that there was an increasing number of middle-class Negroes; they had checking accounts and were buying homes. Apparently their more stable way of living had changed their tastes and interests. Mr. Johnson revised his editorial policy, building up a more substantial coverage of events. Circulation went up again.

The publisher had found he could profit by discovering the new American Negro. White America will begin to solve the housing integration problem to the nation's profit when, like Mr. Johnson, it looks around and learns what the Negro is like today.

6 · Struggle for Decent Jobs

> We are told to prepare, but we see half-prepared whites getting ahead. We are told to learn, but our children are carefully, technically and administratively shunted to certain schools. We are told to be diligent on the job, but we are denied promotion.
>
> —Roy Wilkins

If one looks at the segment of industry the writers know best, mass communications, he sees the sharp and sickening contrast between ideals and reality in Negro employment. Editorial writers assail employers for not hiring Negroes, urge politicians to do more and criticize Negroes for lacking gumption to get training. Yet the American newspaper is one of the most segregated institutions in American life.

Before 1960, there were probably no more than a dozen Negro editorial workers in the daily "white" press of the United States.[1] In the last few years, more have been employed, and a newspaper may now proudly show off its Negro reporter as proof of liberality (somewhat as an "integrated" church may, embarrassingly, point to one Negro member as proof of Christian brotherhood).

Some editors now appeal to journalism schools for Negro

---

[1] Negro printers and ad salesmen are also rare. Magazines are more segregated than newspapers.

employees. Their purpose may be "to get one before it's forced," as a metropolitan photographer put it to us, or to find someone who can cover interracial news. Few seem to consider a Negro reporter as simply a newspaperman who might be asked to report any story needed. There are not many Negroes in journalism for the same reason that not many Negroes are studying to be lawyers or scientists or accountants; in part it may be lack of money or know-how or ambition, but the chief reason is that for decades the employment door has been closed. Why study for newspaper work if the only job you can get is sweeping the newsroom floor?

The picture is changing. The American Newspaper Guild recently estimated that there are about a hundred Negro editorial workers on U.S. dailies, ten having been employed by the *Toledo Blade* in the first half of 1964. Many white editors would still not think of employing Negro writers, but the field is opening. An increased number of Negro students could usefully enter journalism schools today. The jobs will be there for them—and for Negro scientists and lawyers and accountants and business executives—because the white power structure of the nation is waking up!

It will be a long time, however, before the schooling of Negroes improves enough to feed large numbers into college and the professions. Meantime, there's great need to give suitable jobs to those with limited education, and to promote them fairly when they earn it. Only by doing so can the white community answer the cry of a bitter Negro father who spoke out at a recent meeting in the North: "I love my kids and my wife as much as you love yours . . . and sometimes I sit home and cry because I see my white friends doing so much better than I, with the same education I have."

One of the big tasks we face is to open up jobs for "or dinary" Negroes. As Louis Lomax says, "This is what th struggle is all about—Negroes want the right to be ordi nary." There are still many "ordinary" jobs, requiring n very lengthy or special training beyond high school, tha are virtually closed to Negroes. For example, it's seldor that one sees Negro route men or driver salesmen for th foodstuffs delivered to markets and homes. You can't sa we're not qualified—we've been driving limousines for Mr Charlie for years.

An employer cannot allow himself to shrug, "No Negroe ever have applied." Among whites, girls think twice abou becoming engineers because of male predominance in th engineering field. Likewise, Negroes are unlikely to see an purpose in preparing themselves for fields in which white have a monopoly.

What progress, if any, has been made with jobs?

In 1961, the late President Kennedy created a federa Committee on Equal Employment Opportunity, and on of its recent reports stated that corrective action had bee taken in regard to about half of the 5,200 complaints re ceived against employers. Between 1961 and 1963, thoug white-collar employment rose about 2 percent, such em ployment of Negroes went up 17.4 percent. And AFL-CIO unions were "accelerating their union programs for fai practices," the committee reported.

One complicating factor in the situation is that automa tion is tightening employment opportunities for worker: both Negro and white, in a number of fields. As jobs be come scarcer, the plight of the Negro will become wors unless adjustments are made in union and employer prac tices. Yet job scarcity is apt to increase the opposition c white workers to an equitable distribution of such jobs a exist. Thus the problem enlarges into one of finding ways to provide full employment.

The Negro today generally gets poorer jobs and lower wages. Even in the federal government, for example, the Negro is largely restricted to lower-echelon jobs. The advisory committee of the U. S. Commission on Civil Rights reported recently that the 59,832 Negro employees in the District of Columbia area represented about a quarter of the total federal payroll there—but only 1.3 percent of those were in the higher grades, 12 through 18.

"We are still faced with the problem of qualified Negro young people who continue to find some doors closed to them," the committee report said. It added that 10 percent of white youths looking for jobs were unable to find them but for non-whites the figure was 47 percent.

When Negroes do get jobs, they are generally paid less. The average Negro earns only about half the average income for whites.

"There is a continuing lag and it is getting worse," Secretary of Labor W. Willard Wirtz said recently in a radio interview. He reported that average hourly earnings of whites have gone up from $1.90 to $3.20 since 1949, but Negro earnings in the meantime have risen from $1.00 to only $1.75.

Senator Hubert H. Humphrey pointed out similarly that in 1962 the average white man's income was $5,462. Average Negro income was $3,023. A Negro college graduate, he reported, can expect to earn $185,000 in his lifetime; but a white can earn $191,000—with only an *eighth grade education!*

When a Negro gets an unusually good job, therefore, it is news. It was a front page story in New York, for example, when Mrs. Anne M. Roberts was named to the $22,500 position of antipoverty director. The line of advance moves

unsteadily; one city may trail another by twenty-five year
in opening certain positions to Negroes.

Not long ago, two elderly New York Negroes were hon
ored at a Harlem celebration as the "first" in their fields
Both now retired, they are Samuel J. Battle, eighty-one
who was the city's first Negro policeman when he joinec
the force in 1911, and Wesley Williams, sixty-seven, firs
Negro fireman, named in 1919. Mr. Battle rose to lieutenan
and Mr. Williams to battalion chief. Now there are 1,30
Negro policemen and 600 firemen in the city. After th
1964 riots, Capt. Lloyd G. Sealy was named as the firs
Negro to command a precinct in Harlem.

Only recently did New York get its first Negro principa
of a junior high school, Mrs. Edythe Gaines, one of seve
children of a Protestant Episcopal minister. Married to a
electronics engineer, she has a master's degree from Nev
York University and is working on a doctorate at Harvarc

There were other "firsts" recently, even in Dixie. In the 422
man force in Richmond, Virginia, a Negro policeman wa
promoted to lieutenant. In Houston, a Negro was namec
substitute City Court judge and became the first Negr
judge in Texas. Leslie N. Shaw, named postmaster of Lo
Angeles in September, 1964, became the first Negro to ge
such a position in a major city.

Notable changes have been coming even in business
Jackie Robinson, first Negro to play league baseball, wa
personnel director for Chock Full o' Nuts lunch counters
and when he resigned, he was replaced by another Negrc
Herbert Samuel. E. Fred Morrow, who was an administra
tive assistant to President Eisenhower, has been appointec
an assistant vice president of the world's largest privately
owned bank, the Bank of America in San Francisco. U. S
Industries, Inc., a manufacturing company whose customer
and employees are primarily white, named to its board

Negro lawyer, Samuel R. Pierce Jr., a Phi Beta Kappa and Cornell Law School graduate. Chosen for the board of the chain store W. T. Grant was Asa T. Spaulding, the president of an insurance company, the largest Negro-owned business in the nation. Two Negroes have been elected to a board of a major Washington bank, and seven Negroes with top managerial positions were honored at a New York dinner recently.

The changing attitude toward Negro employment is illustrated also by the New York World's Fair, whose exhibitors crowed about the large number of Negroes employed. A cynic might say it was mostly for show. But one exhibitor declared: "The World's Fair represents the attitude of American business today. They all want to improve job opportunities for members of minority groups."

Recruiting at Negro colleges, the exhibitors employed high proportions of Negroes among their hosts and hostesses: General Electric, 10 out of 110; General Motors, 19 out of 38; Ford, 26 out of 200; DuPont, 8 out of 45.

Syracuse, cited earlier, is probably a typical city in the degree of progress it has made in employing Negroes. Here are figures on Negro employment recently reported by the mayor: five policemen, five firemen, forty teachers, five physicians on a project at St. Joseph's Hospital.

In addition to several Negro engineers at the General Electric plant in that city there are a vice principal, a psychiatrist with the State Mental Health Clinic, a county research director, a reporter, a staff director with the Council of Churches, and a gynecologist.

Such figures raise the question of whether one or five Negroes represents justice for the minority. Just what is the fair number? The answer probably is that the numbers game should be avoided and skin color overlooked in hiring. But that is for Utopia. In tense hiring situations, both

whites and Negroes have strong ideas about how many Ne
groes, if any, should be employed.

Often it is a real break-through when the first Negr
fireman or engineer or professor is named. Sometimes, how
ever, this is mere "tokenism." Whites have a way of citing
a single Negro employee as a sign of progress and tolerance
and the Negro may say cynically, "Oh, I'm their Negro."

The aim of job integrationists is to increase the numbe
beyond a mere token. Negroes want their fair share. Man
feel that if one-tenth of a population is Negro and there ar
100 jobs in an office, a quota of ten jobs should go t
Negroes.

There is pressure also to go beyond quota proportions
Not long ago these were insistent demands that Negroe
be preferred in hiring, in order that the historic injustic
of job discrimination be balanced. This brought a reactio
from threatened white workers charging discrimination i
reverse. They expressed fear that Negroes are "takin
over."

In the decades ahead, all of us, both Negroes and whites
shall probably have to tolerate degrees of integration tha
displease us. Goodwill is essential as we work toward th
time when widespread job opportunities become a realit
for Negroes and color is *really* forgotten in hiring and fir
ing.

During this period of transition, whites will need to mak
a gingerly approach to their responsibilities. Because i
most instances whites now dispense jobs, the Negro natur
ally expects whites to open the way to better employment
But as the white man seeks to help a Negro get training o
a particular job, he may be despicably paternalistic. Eve
if he is innocent of paternalism, he may be suspected of it
So too, the Negro who accepts a white hand may be charge
with Uncle Tomism, especially by the soul-damaged youn

Negro who, like his delinquent white counterpart, would rather be resentful than employed. Both whites and Negroes who want to overcome job discrimination will have to experiment with loving kindness as they look at each other's peculiar posture during these months and years when tokenism is both progress and a dirty word.

Americans have reacted to job discrimination with protest and action. Demonstrators have chained themselves to cranes and sat in roadways and dumped garbage. After the Rochester riots, the president of the NAACP there cited jobs for newcomers to the city as a major requirement of racial peace.

One of the most dramatic protests on job discrimination was made by a minister. The Rev. Donald S. Harrington of the Community Church (Unitarian-Universalist) in New York "sat down in a puddle of mud" during a group demonstration at the World's Fair opening. When the ministers and others were arrested, he explained it was "a deliberate act of civil disobedience in the tradition of Henry David Thoreau, Mahatma Gandhi and Martin Luther King," and his board of trustees approved it "with admiration."

But weren't fair exhibitors trying to be just to the Negro?

Dr. Harrington said that the fair, which was "proclaimed to be a portent of peace through understanding, was actually built by labor unions still, in fact, largely segregated and in which there is as yet neither peace nor understanding of the issue of human brotherhood."

The National Urban League, the rights organization most concerned about employment, has a new plan of finding qualified Negroes and maintaining a "skills bank," which employers can draw on. In the first six months of the program, the League reported, 1,700 Negroes were placed.

To cite one example of this program's effectiveness: In the first half of 1963, the Urban League of Essex County

in New Jersey placed only fifty Negroes in good jobs. In
the same period the next year, with a skills bank, the total
was 376! The placements included not only unskilled and
semiskilled workers but also engineers and clerks. The seven
fold increase, a leader reported, "was due largely to
general improvement in the attitudes of employers toward
Negroes."

In Newark, New Jersey, a Business and Industrial Coor
dinating Committee, organized to develop integration of
the labor market, helped find jobs for more than 4,000
Negro and Puerto Rican workers in 1963-4. This was a
third of the new workers hired in the year by the hundred
organizations represented in the group.

A major recent step to promote integrated employment
was the passage of the civil rights act of 1964. Its Title
VII created an Equal Employment Opportunity Committee.
This body is to investigate complaints, seek to persuade
where it finds discrimination and, if necessary, sue in the
federal courts. Some states have, of course, long had fair
employment laws with similar goals.

It is often argued that laws will not change minds; there
is truth in this, though laws have persuasive force on many
people, especially those on the fence. There have been not
fewer than five important actions since the spring of 1964,
however, to use education and social pressure rather than
law to improve Negro opportunities.

1. The Urban League announced a reorganization and ex
pansion "to combat poverty and despair" and established three
new regional offices. Projects being developed aim to reduce
school drop-outs, increase youth motivation, and expand re
training.

2. The President's committee mentioned above is now try
ing to establish a relationship between Negro colleges and
major corporations. The aim: To help Negro graduates get

good jobs. Some Negro colleges have never been in contact with business and industry. Now they will be.

3. An interracial Council for Business Opportunity has launched a program to encourage Negroes to start their own businesses. The number in businesses for themselves is at present small. In Harlem, for example, only 18 percent of the retail stores are owned by Negroes; one reason is that Negroes have often not known how to go about getting technical advice from banks. The American Jewish Congress and the Urban League are co-sponsors of the program.

4. The AFL-CIO—in spite of the white backlash among many workmen—approved a program to reach the employment goals of the civil rights act. Since some employers say that they would hire Negroes if union officials would let them, one major goal of the new AFL-CIO plan is to educate workers about the new act. The union leaders also plan to include fair employment practices in their negotiations of new contracts.

5. The National Association of Manufacturers sent a vice president, Charles A. Kothe of Tulsa, Oklahoma, around the country to conduct seminars on the civil rights act and educate 16,000 NAM members for compliance with the spirit of this law.

What is the role of the churches in job discrimination? In August, 1964, the United Church of Christ issued a booklet recommending that members write letters, buy selectively, and if necessary, demonstrate nonviolently to assure fair employment. The following month the National Catholic Conference announced that it would begin a two-year program to use Catholic purchasing power to fight job discrimination.

Following such leadership, could not individual churchmen do more about employment? Could not our religiously-motivated business and professional men do more, cooperatively, to establish projects for scholarships, training, recruiting, and placement in the sectors of economic life that they control? Does fear make them hesitate, or apathy?

"Our problem," said Whitney M. Young, Jr., executive director of the Urban League, in discussing Negro employment, "has been not that of ill-will or goodwill but that of no will."

If a bare majority of the business and professional men in our churches and synagogues replaced apathy with vigorous goodwill, most Negro complaints related to jobs could be scotched by 1970.

7 · Struggle for Modern Schools

> Psychological studies have shown that the Negro child in America becomes convinced at an early age that he is inferior because of the color of his skin. What this really means is that the Negro becomes prejudiced against himself at the start of life by accepting the white man's prejudice against him.
> —Dr. Benjamin Spock

There are two major counts against school segregation: the harm it does to the schooling of Negro children, and the damage it wreaks on the American psyche.

"Negroes are on the verge of a major economic crisis," *Fortune* magazine declared recently, "for the gap is widening between Negro education and training on the one hand, and the requirements of the labor market, on the other." Unhappily, Negroes could win full civil rights and still be, on the whole, too poorly educated to get a decent job. Or as one Negro leader has said, the Negro masses could end "with a mouthful of rights, living in hovels, with empty stomachs."

The psychological damage is worked on both Negro and white child. Some whites are sensitive to this. A waiting list soon developed after the child of Ralph Bunche, the American Negro diplomat, was enrolled in a Quaker school; it was explained that white parents were eager to have their boys and girls grow up in the "one world" atmosphere of the school.

Unfortunately, not all parents have this vision. Eleven-year-old Hugh Lomax, son of Louis Lomax, the noted writer, ran into a solid barrier when he tried to enroll at a Long Island military academy. The headmaster explained to Mrs. Lomax that the school had enrolled two Negro boys some years ago but they had been ostracized. He added that there were no single rooms available and "it would be difficult to get the other boys to sleep with him." Of course, the school had "no policy against" Negroes! The tragedy in such a situation is that the spirits of both Negro and white boys are warped.

When the Negro student James Meredith was admitted to the University of Mississippi, a chemistry professor invited him to dinner. A bigot retaliated against the professor's grade school daughter. When her class exchanged gifts at a school Christmas tree, she received a Negro rag doll with a card: "Nigger lover." And this in commemoration of the birth of Jesus! Segregation strikes at white children by distorting their values.

Dr. Benjamin Spock, the famous pediatrician whose *Baby and Child Care* has sold into the millions, has warned that "the harm to adults and children which results from segregation is increasing steadily." In a "lay sermon" during the Washington prayer services for civil rights, Dr. Spock declared that discrimination "is harmful to white children" as well as to Negro children, whom it "undermines." The prejudice the Negro child absorbs is expressed, Dr. Spock said, "in low expectations for himself in school and career." The Negro child comes to think less well of his family, his friends and his race, and in turn they hold him in lower esteem. Dr. Joseph S. Himes, North Carolina College sociologist, describes the process as "learned apathy." Deprived parents tend to suppress their children's spontaneity unintentionally, he says, because it may be threatening or dangerous.

"What is the difference if the Negro learns in his own segregated school?" asks the white parent. The difference is that neither white nor Negro child gets a first-hand school experience of brotherhood. Put another way, both absorb the anti-Christian doctrine that living as brothers is all right in theory or Bible verses but not in practice.

The Rev. Oliver Brown, a 33-year-old assistant pastor of an A.M.E. church in Topeka, Kansas, found a notice in his door one day that his daughter should register at a school four blocks away. "I guess," he recalls, "the school officials didn't know we were Negroes." For when he took nine-year-old Linda to register, she was turned down. Though she lived in a white neighborhood and played with white children, she was told she must go to a Negro school twenty-one blocks away. The pastor reported this to the NAACP, and the organization started suit.

That was in 1952. Two years later, the U.S. Supreme Court ruled for Linda—which was of course the famous ruling that started the end of school segregation.

Almost a decade after the Topeka rebuff, Mr. Brown, who meantime had become a pastor in Springfield, Missouri, proudly told about Linda's good scholastic record and explained: "I want her to have something more to look forward to than washing dishes." Linda herself explained that she wanted to study music and start her own teaching studio.

Since the 1954 decision, school integration has gone ahead slowly, despite resistance that has occasionally resulted in violence. Some churches have given leadership in educating for integration. When nine Negroes entered the first grades of Houston, Texas, the Episcopal bishop, the

Rt. Rev. John E. Hines, recently elected presiding bishop of his denomination, wrote a letter asking members of the church there to act "as becomes men and women to whom Jesus Christ gave life and freedom."

One of the most widely-publicized programs to bring school integration with a minimum of shock to public opinion was in Dallas, Texas, the last big city of the state to yield on the issue. The movement started at the top when a committee was appointed from the city's white power structure, referred to in Chapter 2, to meet with a committee of Negro representatives. The whites were all active church laymen of local congregations, and two of the Negroes were clergymen. They met more than fifty times over a period of eighteen months. Posters and leaflets were prepared. A special movie was shown to a thousand church groups and other organizations, and ministers preached on Christian responsibility in race relations. As a result, first-grade integration began in 1961, without incident, and in the words of a *Christian Century* correspondent, the city felt inwardly "something akin to a religious experience."

New Orleans had gone through bitter weeks as its schools integrated the year before, but courageous clergymen helped overcome resistance. When white parents boycotted the schools, a white Methodist, the Rev. Lloyd A. Foreman, braved taunting women to take his five-year-old daughter to class. As a result, creosote-filled light bulbs were tossed at his church, and when he preached, four women walked out.

"If it hadn't been for that nigger-lover, we'd have won our fight," said one.

At the start of the 1964-5 school year, the Roman Catholic bishop of Mississippi ordered desegregation of first-grade classes in parochial schools. That same year, three Negro children, entering a red building at Biloxi, became the first

Negroes to attend public schools in Mississippi. Three Southern capitals—Jackson, Montgomery and Columbus—desegregated at least one district. These were among 113 school districts that accepted a few Negroes for the first time, including 4 each in Mississippi and Alabama, 25 each in Virginia and Texas, and 22 in North Carolina. About one in four school districts in the South now has some integration.

But if there was some reason for satisfaction, the militant egalitarian found progress very minor after ten years. At the Little Rock Central High School, only 33 Negroes had been placed among the 2,100 whites under the slow operations of its assignment plan (though a Negro girl, graduated there with highest honors in 1964, was named a presidential scholar.) Meantime, three Negroes were graduated from once-white schools in Birmingham. The first Negro was graduated from a desegregated school in Tampa, Florida. Baton Rouge, Louisiana, graduated twenty-eight Negroes from four desegregated schools.

These illustrations have been taken from the South because that is where the court decision required open steps to change segregation patterns. In the North, the pattern has been a bit different. Here school segregation is *de facto* —that is, it exists in fact if not in law, because neighborhoods are largely segregated. To make matters worse, school boards have sometimes gerrymandered districts to reduce even the small amount of integration that would be "normal."

Officials and civil rights leaders have tackled this problem in different ways. In New York state, for example, the education commissioner ordered the end of "racial imbalance." In some places this meant bussing pupils from one area to another. Despite the fact the busses have been used for decades in farm and suburban areas, not to mention parochial districts, some white parents objected strenuously to the bussing plan. "The neighborhood school" became a rallying slogan, with the sudden emotional appeal of flag and mother.

In New York City in 1964, in an effort to force an end to *de facto* segregation, Negroes boycotted the schools, then agreed to approve a Board of Education plan for integration —whereupon whites organized to fight it. A white boycott kept some children out of school temporarily when classes started in the fall.

Some Northern cities turned to "the Princeton Plan" as a model. In 1948, Princeton, New Jersey, with a ghetto of about 1,200 Negroes, had integrated 120 children from a Negro school with 580 pupils in a nearby white school. Both were good schools and they were close enough to each other that transportation was no problem. So one school took all the children of both races from the first through the fifth grade, and the other, all those from the sixth grade through the eighth.

Negroes complained later, however, that Princeton's integration plan did not bring about automatic improvement of the Negroes' situation in the community. The job outlook did not improve. Only in more recent years has Princeton made real progress.

A Princeton Negro pointed up a problem that arises in many Northern schools that Negroes and whites attend together, without understanding each other, when he said: "We were lazy. We were apathetic. We were the ones who made the discipline problems. That's what a lot of people were saying, and the awful thing we had to face was that there was some truth in it.

"What they didn't understand is what it does to a person always to be belittling himself—to be told or shown every day that he is less than a man. Oh, Princetonians didn't put it that way, but it came through. And after you had heard it often enough, you suspected that it might be true, and finally things got hopeless and you stopped trying."

Speaking of the limitations at Princeton, Dean Alex Rosen of the School of Social Work, New York University, pointed out that integration should be a continuous movement: "Desegregation moves toward integration as the program of the school is self-consciously and deliberately organized so that Negro and white children modify their attitudes toward one another; as the children come to enjoy equal status; as teachers learn to understand the Negro child, and as the opportunity structure is opened for better jobs and housing."

That is the way it ought to be.

It is often said that the Negro lacks an educational tradition, and slavery and segregation are blamed for this. So tradition must be created for the Negro child.

The place to begin is to give the Negro his place in recorded history. Recognizing Negroes in America's past would do much to erase the Negro's invisibility. A number of textbook publishers are issuing revised and corrected history books to give belated recognition to the Negroes' contributions to the development of this country. The New York State Department of Education has an excellent intercultural education section, headed by Mrs. Nida Thomas, which offers free a variety of resources about the contributions of minority groups.

Few people are aware that the Negro has made significant contributions in America. The first person to die in the American Revolution, the first person to operate on a human heart, the inventors of the brown paper bag and the machine for stitching shoe soles to the uppers—all these were Negroes. How many whites can name them? Or for that matter, how many Negroes? Negro children often grow up unaware that they, too, are descended from makers of America's history.

Check yourself—do you know what part Benjamin Banneker, Matthew Henson, John Russwurm, Richard Allen, Phillis Wheatley and Harriet Tubman played in our history?

Negro leaders should insist that Negro youth stay in school. Negro parents must inform themselves about the procedures of the school system so that they can help their children fit into it even as they help change its structure. At the same time, they must make it clear that the rights of the Negro are due him now, and that he is not studying in an attempt to earn these rights or to prove himself worthy of them.

The militant integrationist has given a low priority to Negro education, as distinguished from school integration, for he must avoid seeming to agree with the segregationist who says: "Let the Negroes get an education and demonstrate that they are ready."

The militant pushes for an end to de facto *segregated schools almost as if this alone would stop the forces that years of segregation have set into motion: retarded reading and mathematics skills, low motivation, low aspiration.*

Many school people are more keenly aware of the hurdles to be overcome in helping children learn than either segregationists or militants. The size of the school organization mitigates against rapid turn-on-a-dime changes in direction. The sums of money needed to replace textbooks with revisions; the time needed, running into years, for really adequate revisions to be made; the money for bussing the children around the city; the training and retraining of teachers in the new directions; the recruitment of enough remedial-reading and arithmetic teachers to help children who started

*out in inferior schools or in disadvantaged home situations
—these are considerations the schoolman must face.*

*When he points to some of the difficulties, he is accused
of moving too slowly. If he attempts to set up special programs in the more deprived sections of the city, he runs the
risk of having those who would postpone integration use
these programs as an excuse for waiting. The militant integrationist meanwhile denounces the program as a "separate
but equal" device.*

What is needed is a frank look at the educational process.
Civil rights leaders need to sit down with educators in an
atmosphere of mutual trust to seek workable solutions.
White parents must be willing to weigh special interests
against the loss of human potential. Civil rights leaders must
be willing to concede that bussing or the Princeton plan
may not be the best or only answers. Where they are, white
parents need to organize to help integrate rather than to
boycott. Negro parents must become more deeply interested
in school policies.

If the entire community is mobilized, meaningful changes
can be made, changes that will result in better education for
all children.

Work must also be done to bring full college integration.
The Supreme Court some years ago extended to tax-sup-
ported colleges the integration principle enunciated in Linda
Brown's case; headlines documented the more dramatic
aspects of desegregation at major Southern universities.
But Negroes have not been flooding colleges that accept
them. "White" institutions have to encourage them to enroll. The Jesuits of New York have asked their high schools
and colleges to "seek out" acceptable Negroes. Princeton
University, which made an appeal to 4,000 high schools for
Negro students, got 13 among the 800 in its new class of

1968. Cornell University has a full-time staff member hunting qualified Negroes, but its 1964-5 freshman class has only 16 out of 2,500. If Negroes are to attend college in any considerable numbers, planning must evidently start much earlier.

"We must go way down below the junior and senior years in high school," said Cornell's president, Dr. James A. Perkins. "The seventh and eighth grades are the critical levels and the next big effort likely to yield immediate results will come there."

Churches and business groups could find ways to help Negro youngsters set their sights on college. This raising of goals is one of the good byproducts of primary and secondary school integration. But it's well for churchmen to remember that brotherhood does not always develop naturally; it can use cultivation. The self-segregation of students in integrated high schools proves how an older generation's stereotypes can carry over. Fortunately, reality breaks through sometimes, and this is why even a poor integrated school is better than a good one that is "separate but equal."

Dr. Robert Coles, a Harvard psychiatrist, has found that Negro children placed in newly integrated schools have suffered pain but "survived successfully." He went to once-embattled New Orleans expecting to find such children suffering from psychological injury, but discovered that what he had considered "a stress" was exactly the opposite, "a challenge to them."

"Even if there are only one or two Negroes in a school, the white children learn things about them that they otherwise never would have," says Dr. Coles.

"For a Negro to answer a question in a math class conflicts with the white stereotype of the Negro. And when a Negro child is called on in class and does not know the answer, and a white child does not know the answer either, it creates a bond between them."

Without in any sense holding it up as a model, let's look again at Syracuse to see in concrete detail how a Northern city comes to grips with racial change. With an influx from the South, the Negro population has zoomed (from 5,000 to 12,000 during the fifties). Since Negro families are large and young here, Negro children account for about 13 percent of the school population. But the majority of them attend two grade schools, which are about four-fifths Negro; one junior high is 78 percent Negro.

What life is like for a Negro youngster in Syracuse was described in the *Syracuse Post-Standard* by reporter Edwin K. Wiley, himself a Negro:

> Unless his family can get into public housing, he may well live in a substandard dwelling. He will probably attend the city's poorer schools, and be surrounded in his everyday neighborhood life by persons of questionable character . . . College is financially out of the question for him, and chances are he will quit school when he is 16 because he really doesn't see any advantage in finishing. After all, he can find work as some kind of unskilled laborer, and if not, welfare will take care of him . . . .

Syracuse has tried to overcome educational shortcomings for the Negro in two major ways—through an enrichment program in the ghetto and by taking steps to overcome imbalance in the schools.

The enrichment program, known as the Madison Area Project, was set up in three slum-area schools—a compensatory program to overcome the disadvantages of underprivileged children, including many Negroes. Changes were made in the daily school program, not only in what was taught but how. Teachers received special training, specialists aided in such areas as remedial reading, and 200 volunteers helped with tutoring and clubs. Field trips were added, and materials more meaningful to these children were employed. Community agencies, business and government joined hands to do the job.

The project became a catalyst for other solutions too. A graduate program in urban teaching was set up in co-operation with Syracuse University. An intercultural relations team was organized to provide supporting services to children who transferred from project schools; one aim was to help the schools to which they moved develop real integration and thus prevent the flight of whites to the suburbs.

In 1963 the President's Committee on Juvenile Delinquency granted Syracuse funds to seek answers to the problems of delinquency, dependancy and drop-outs in slum areas. A large cross section of the population of the survey areas, including many Negroes, was recruited for the task forces in education, employment and community services. Survey of needs were made, plans formed, and as a result, enrichment of the Madison type is being extended to these other "action areas."

So Syracuse is starting. Many other cities have the same opportunity. The Ford Foundation has launched a Great Cities program to help the culturally deprived. Sixteen other cities besides Syracuse received grants from the President's committee, and the new Anti-Poverty program promises to aid communities wishing to attack problems related to the poor and their education.

Education is the bridge to the future for all of us. One suspects that some Negro leaders are willing to discount the present generation, seeing school integration as a hope for the next. But the present generation produces the next. All the studies show that school drop-outs breed drop-outs. Welfare families are now producing the fourth generation of welfare recipients. It is wishful thinking to feel that the children in a segregated school, who at twelve years read at fourth grade level (because in the primary grades they were taught with middle-class-oriented publications meaningless to them) will catch up simply because they are taken to another school. Negro leaders have to face this fact and call for special help for these children.

The steps to reduce imbalance in Syracuse have included closing old schools, redistricting and some bussing of Negroes to less crowded schools that were largely white. Civil rights groups, while asking that the program go further, have generally gone along with it.

Another *Post-Standard* writer, Miss Eleanor Rosebrugh, a social worker and Unitarian leader, described how one of the first steps worked out—bussing seventy sixth graders from Merrick School, which was overcrowded and predominantly Negro, to Roberts school two miles away.

The Negro parents at first did not like the idea of bussing. White parents at Roberts were disturbed and wondered whether the Negro children could keep up.

What in fact happened? Mrs. Helen Sheridan, the Roberts principal, reported "restlessness at times" among the children from Merrick. Sometimes the white children called the Negroes names. However: "Some of this year's top students were from Merrick," the principal said. "Many were very bright, and most were very well cared for."

The Negro children presented no more disciplinary problems "than any other children," she reported. Negro parents were cooperative. One Negro boy was a fire lieutenant, two entered an "excel" program.

What was the reaction of white parents?

"My child benefited from acquaintance with the Merrick children," said one Roberts mother.

Another said: "There was no drop academically. And anyway, anything they might have failed to learn from books would have been compensated for by learning more about people."

Education definitely has a place in the struggle for decency, a prominent one. But the need for education must be dissociated from any "go slow" connotations it may have gathered. Improved education must not be considered a prerequisite to giving the Negro his rights. But the schools must be organized so that all children can profit. The benefits will be reaped not only by Negroes but by America and the whole world. Who can say whether the discoverer of the cure for cancer will be a once-deprived American Negro, a white from Appalachia, a Chinese, or a Nigerian? And how can we measure the stretching of spirit that comes to white Anglo-Saxons whose value system was changed as a result of contact with children of other groups during their school days?

8 · *Violence Versus Nonviolence*

> We have required a superhuman patience of the
> American Negro, and when this has proved too much
> for his tortured person, we have been dismayed be-
> cause he has answered with an excess of agitation.
> —Cardinal Cushing

Negroes have been throwing rocks and bottles and
Molotov cocktails and overturning cars and attacking
whites. And that spells: violence!

As the months and years of the sixties have passed, there
has been a rising cry that violence would come. Finally in
various cities violence did explode, and it will explode
again.

For many whites the analysis was simple: It shows that
Negroes are wild animals not ready for freedom; so suppress
them. If it were that simple, the chapter could end here.
But this logic ignores the fact that white people have been
violent with night sticks and fire hoses and police dogs and
shotguns and ropes. Moreover, the violence of the Hiroshima
bombing and the Nazi concentration camps and the Communist purges was predominantly white. Must we conclude,
then, that whites are wild animals not ready for freedom?

Meeting Negro violence with curfews and troopers in an
emotional binge of backlash is neither logical nor workable,

except possibly for very short periods. We must move quickly to understand what causes the violence and to attack those causes.

The headlines have also carried news of nonviolent civil rights offensives "in the streets": picketings and marches and sit-ins and acts of civil disobedience such as lying before trucks. These actions seem close to lawlessness. Don't they lead to violence? Don't they stir up to riots? Don't Negroes have to stop all this agitation before we can have racial peace?

To get perspective on these questions, we have to understand that, however incredible it may seem to some staid church members, these actions stem from the teachings of Jesus and specifically from the Sermon on the Mount.

If we take literally the dictums "turn the other cheek" and "resist not evil," we may turn to pure nonresistance of the perfectionist Tolstoyan type. But most white Christians do not accept this radical interpretation, as witnessed by generations that have opposed forces represented by the Kaiser and Tojo and Mao.

But a second interpretation of the Bible teaching on non-violence, not quite so radical, permits nonviolent direct action (often miscalled "passive resistance" since it is dynamic and not passive). This was perfected by Gandhi, who called it *Satyagraha*. Many times the story has been told of how he shaped his ideas from Thoreau's "Civil Disobedience" and the Sermon on the Mount. And in time the British imperialists quit India. "Nonviolence," as the technique came to be called, worked!

The influence of Gandhi's thought on Martin Luther King Jr. is direct and clear. Both the Negro leaders James Farmer and Bayard Rustin came out of the American pacifist movement, for which Gandhi has long been a saint. CORE sprang from the heart of the church-generated Fellowship of Reconciliation, the nation's major pacifist organization (both Farmer and Rustin were once employees of FOR, an association that is significant in understanding their philosophy).

Has Christian pacifism borne racial war?

In the sense that it has bared conflicts, yes. But what are the alternatives? One alternative is to ignore the conflicts, which is what most white people appear ready to do. The white racist hothead tries to obliterate the conflict with electric cattle-prods and high-power firehoses. The Negro racist hothead would obliterate the conflict by erasing his white opponents. Avoiding such unreal or unchristian solutions, the philosophy of nonviolence seeks to overcome conflict by peaceful confrontation and reconciliation. It attempts to use the power of self-sacrificing love in what has been called moral jiu-jitsu.

Nonviolence requires training and intense discipline. Churches in the South have been schools to train young Negro nonviolent actionists to resist being provoked even by brutality, to try to love those who persecute them. And since the time has been so short and the teachers so few, the wonder is that nonviolence has been as successful as it has. The technique can get out of hand. It did in India, and Gandhi went on long fasts to bring his followers back to his philosophy. Martin Luther King himself has said it is no cure-all.

Is it ever moral to break the law? The argument against the morality of nonviolent resistance to laws implies that the moral order is on the side of human law. Some would say that God, supporting the State, endorses laws approved by men. Others, leaving God aside, have the emotional conviction that law has the weight of divine order. But these are naive and idolatrous attitudes. Man is not God, and his ever-shifting rules have no eternal sanction.

A much more persuasive argument is that open violation of law tends to create disrespect for law, just as running through a red light does; and general disrespect would result in anarchy and lawlessness; and a broken society would of course tend to make all immoralities easier. This is not easily answered, and ultimately nonviolent protesters have to answer it with the moral weight of their lives. They are, by and large, the most rigid and even Puritanical of men, and so symbolically their violation is quite different from ordinary violations. Its meaning is quite different from the violation, for example, by the segregationist landlord in his substandard housing. Ironically, his illegal activity is seldom assailed as undermining the moral foundations of American society, since it is a part of the American status quo we wink at so easily. We simply don't think of discrimination as a crime in the way burglary is. Because of the unique, witnessing character of nonviolent demonstrations, the planned and purposeful violation of human law tends to validate law in general. Selection of the unjust law underscores the justice of laws in general.

The argument for the open, purposeful violation of law is a plain one. It is not that the end of integration validates it, as some suppose; the end does not justify the means. Rather, the rationale is related to conscience and all its subleties and possible illusions. If one must choose, one follows the divine laws as one sees them rather than the laws made by finite and fallible men. In the old phrase: Obey God rather than man. Those pallid words still embody a revolutionary doctrine, as many a grubby jail cell still testifies.

But isn't violating a law for conscience' sake a kind of setting oneself up as the final judge—as God himself? Yes, in a way, of course. Those who engage in nonviolent resistance to unjust laws should recognize that they may err;

even more subtly, they may fall into smugness and self-satisfaction, idolizing their own neurotic needs rather than praising God.

But that is no new moral threat, nor one unique to demonstrations for interracial justice. Every Christian who makes a moral choice has to rely ultimately on conscience. Whenever he draws lines or weighs relative values, in his business dealings or his personal relationships or his political decisions, he has to depend on his understanding of religious commandments. If he takes religion into account in his decisions, he has to rely on his own finite grasp of God's will. Even if he simply tries to do what the preacher preaches, inevitably he sets up this moral code as better than others' and falls into the danger of self-exaltation. To others, his choice for conscience may seem foolish or self-righteous, or both. That is the usual choice: One follows his own conscience, or one goes along with the crowd. And it is no doubt precisely because so many of us are used to going along with the crowd that we invest society's way with divine sanctions. We decide that it is "immoral" to violate customs and laws and we bitterly scorn those prophetic souls who act on their higher vision of God's will. But since the time of Jesus and before, the parallel paths of compromise and of Judas turncoating have both been familiar threats.

On the other hand the moralist who is not willing to follow his own conscience gets himself into an unenviable predicament. When he lets others decide his morals, he is like the German who accepted Nazi persecution of the Jews because it was "legal." It may properly be objected that there is a different validity in law imposed by a dictator or oligarchy and a law voted by a majority of the people. But this raises another interesting speculation: How valid is a segregation law in a Southern community where most Negroes, and perhaps a majority of the adult population, cannot vote? Still, majority approval of a law, even if joined in by Negroes, does not give it eternal moral status. Ninety-nine percent of the citizens in a New England town meeting could vote for an action and that would not guarantee its morality—the witches were burned, after all, and overwhelming approval by the Puritan citizenry did not make it moral. Men may legislate in accord with God's will, but they don't necessarily, or even usually.

During World War II, when the Nazis occupied France, steps were taken to herd Jews into cattle cars and ship them off east to death in concentration camps. Here was a drastic confrontation of the immorality of racism, and French Christians had to decide. The young men and women of the French Protestant youth organization, *Cimade*, decided to help the Jews. They hid many of them in a rural chateau in the Huguenot territory of southern France and then smuggled them through the barbed wire and among the border guards into free Switzerland. They did this in moral anguish.

A Frenchman could argue that Hitler's German laws did not apply to him—and yet there was the diabolical legal facade of a Nazi-tinged puppet government in France. And it was a clear violation of Swiss law to sneak people across the border without valid passports. Yet these Frenchmen broke the law in order to help Jews, and American churchmen praised them widely for it. They had chosen to violate man's law and to obey God.

So, pondering these truths, many ministers and priests and rabbis and parishioners will continue to demonstrate and to engage in nonviolent but illegal resistance to unjust segregation laws and customs. Yesterday the place of resistance was a lunch counter; tomorrow it may be a motel or a cathedral.

Unhappily, many Negroes, like many whites, have no faith in Christianity or its preachments about love's power. There are Negroes who agree with the father who buys boxing gloves to teach his son "the manly art of self-defense" so he can "take care of himself" with his fists. They accept the logic of the white politician who wants huge armaments since "the only thing the Communists understand is force"—except that such Negro cynicism is directed at whites.

The *Newsweek* poll cited previously showed that two-thirds of Negroes believe persuasion will help bring equality. Two out of three would join a boycott for rights, and one out of two would picket or go to jail. Such is the potential of nonviolence in the Negro population.

But there is soil too for violence. One in five Negroes think some violence between the races is inevitable. And *Newsweek* said that an "alarming" 22 percent feel that the whites will yield only to force.[1] The *New York Times* found 62 percent believe nonviolence will work, but 7 percent felt that Negroes will have to use violence.

Long before the riots of 1964, the irresistible force of Negro opinion was meeting the immovable object of white opinion. Two of five Negroes, *Newsweek* found, feel white men want to keep them down. But three out of four whites feel the Negro is moving too fast. How racial peace can be maintained when sizable groups of Negroes believe in the antipathy of whites and the need of violence, and whites believe that the Negro should be patient, is not easy to comprehend.

If the force keeps on and the object does not move, violent explosion is inevitable. Walter Lippmann has compared opposition to Negro rights to "pushing on the safety valve

[1] The *Times* poll found an identical 22 percent who favor non-violence but believe violence will occur.

and tying it down." "To stop the protests and to shut off real hope of redressing the grievances is a recipe for disorder," he writes. "If the legitimate grievances of the Negroes cannot be dealt with by open and nonviolent demonstrations and propaganda, a condition will be created for clandestine and violent criminality."

Conservative whites find it easy to feel alarm about Negro hoodlums on subways or Negro rioters. But they have not been so alarmed by the violence to personality of racial injustice. They have perhaps deplored but not become effectively exercised about such incidents in the South as the shooting of Negroes, the bombing of Negro children in church, the beating and murdering of civil rights workers. They have not become righteously furious about such living conditions for Negroes as the following, which were reported by a sociologist in a Northern city:

—A young mother felt it necessary to remain awake at night in a lighted room to protect her newly born child from rats.

—A large family had to live crowded into two rooms because there wasn't enough heat for the entire apartment.

—The children in another family have been hungry at the end of every month because there is not enough money to provide food from one payday to the next.

There is violence here too, a silent violence that is ghastly and white, but rarely does the white opinion leader lash out against it as he does against Negro riots. The Negro may lash out, however, and since no one listens, he may speak violently and even act violently. It is a kind of black backlash to the violent indifference of the majority.

One aspect of the problem of violence is police brutality. There is a futility about arguing police brutality because ordinarily it can no more be proved than payoffs to police for permitting gambling and vice in many cities. Some opinion leaders in such cities, who know that payoffs exist because flagrant vice cannot exist without them, will rush to defend their corrupt police forces against charges of brutality. If there are incidents, they explain, it is because there are always "a few bad apples" on any force. The white community has to refuse to admit the prevalence of brutality because admission would threaten the security structure that provides its whole stability.

But the crucial fact about police brutality is that, whether it can be proved or not, Negroes believe it exists. They simply *know* it exists. In the *New York Times* poll, for example, 31 percent of Negroes said there was some police brutality and 12 percent said "a lot"; only one in five said there was none at all. Writing in the *Nation* Martin Luther King Jr. said:

> The most tragic and widespread violations occur in the areas of police brutality and the enforcement against the Negro of obviously illegal state statutes. For many white Americans in the North there is little comprehension of the grossness of police behavior and its wide practice. The Civil Rights Commission, after a detailed, scholarly and objective study, declared it to be one of the worst manifestations of the Negro's oppression.[2]

In many Northern cities there have been demands for civilian boards, such as that in Philadelphia, to review charges of police brutality. Conservatives argue that the police can't enforce the law if someone is looking over their shoulders, but cynical Negroes view opposition as an effort to help police cover up.

Since Negroes are human, they sometimes do wrong; they may be violent. And they turn to violence for reasons both understandable and obscure. While there are many forms of violence, Negroes who employ violence may be put roughly into two categories—those whose actions are clearly

[2] "Hammer of Civil Rights," in *Nation*, March 9, 1964.

delinquent and criminal, and those whose violence is a social protest against frustration. In condemning Negro violence there should be precision about just what is condemned.

Roy Wilkins, the NAACP leader, attracted wide attention when he wrote a column for a Harlem weekly condemning "teenage Negro hoodlums." He said these "punks" and "foul-mouthed smart alecks" are "undercutting and wrecking gains made by hundreds of Negro and white youngsters who went to jail for human rights." He added the ultimate insult: "These hotshots, tearing up subway cars and attacking innocent people . . . are helping Mississippi."

At the same time, there has been much understanding of the factors leading to violence. Ministers in Harlem preached sermons urging the end of injustice, often using the text from Hosea: "For they have sown the wind, and they shall reap the whirlwind." Ministers and other Negro leaders meeting in Brooklyn riot areas pointed out that riots are "symptoms rather than causes" and resolved: "The basic evils from which the community suffers must be corrected, because the people can no longer be restrained."

Whites drew the same lines of cause and effect. Peter I. Rose, Smith College sociologist, wrote: "The Negroes who live in the urban ghettoes, especially those young people who are uneducated, unskilled, unemployed and—too frequently—unemployable, continue to be embittered by the hopeless environment which is their home and their jail. The violent outbursts of the North are their response."

Such sentiments may be misunderstood as excusing the rioters. On the other hand, statements of condemnation by Negro leaders are seized on as proof that Negroes who turn to violence are in the wrong, so whites can suppress them and relax. But we have two different categories of violence that deserve different interpretation. The crimin-

ality of hoodlums—even if generated by slum life and police brutality—cannot be condoned. But the violent rioting
of frustrated young Negroes, if it cannot be countenanced,
must be understood as a warning. "How else," asked Cardinal Cushing of Boston, "can he answer except in outrage
the society that marks him as inferior to his fellowmen?"

One result of the 1964 riots was that some Negro leaders
urged a moratorium on nonviolent direct action. But fear
of white backlash cannot become the regulator of Negro
agitation. Already many Negroes are moving away from the
old leadership. Small radical groups are proliferating, and
the new leaders that are emerging contend for more drastic
action than Dr. King's nonviolence.

Bayard Rustin has argued that the Negro needs white
allies. He and leaders of the Urban League have urged that
government spend money to provide jobs and get unemployed Negro youths off the sidewalks. The League, seeing
the gap between the leaders and the young masses of Negroes, is frankly trying to establish communication with
the submerged.

The old-line Negro leaders face a virtually impossible
task. They have to get the loyalty of the drop-outs and
deprived who may riot. And somehow, at the risk of being
called Uncle Toms, they have to win the confidence of the
white community in greater measure than they have.

Most whites do not yet grasp that it is revolution and
not evolution that is underway. Perhaps the inch-by-inch
grant of rights cannot be speeded; perhaps, ironically,
rioting will even slow it. But if so, we must be prepared for
more frustration and more violence, more Molotov cocktails
and more police dogs. It will require the dedicated efforts
of Negro leaders and whites of goodwill to get the struggle
for change back on the rails of nonviolent direct action.

PART FOUR

STRUGGLE IN THE CHURCH

9 · *Role of the Negro in the Church*

> We believe that the Church of Jesus Christ is commanded by its Lord to rid itself of all those forms of racial injustice which have been perpetuated through the years by us all in our churches, church organizations, agencies and institutions.
>
> —1963 General Assembly,
> National Council of Churches

Some of the integration problems of jobs and education and even voting come into focus in the churches. This point was made not long ago by the Rev. W. Sterling Cary, moderator of the Congregational churches in New York City. The Negro pastor of an integrated church himself, he argued that the churches are "not without sin" in employment. There is a lack of Negro executives not only in business but in Protestant denominational headquarters. "Theologians talk about the oneness of man," he went on, "but their seminaries steadfastly deny to Negro scholars the right to teach."

The number of highly qualified Negro teachers for seminary jobs, as for other college positions, is very small, explains Dr. John C. Bennett, president of Union Theological Seminary, in *The Christian Century*. "When we build a faculty we have to look for particular persons to fill particular vacancies. If we were looking for professors in general, it would be easier to have the kind of variety in terms of race that seems desirable. Believe me, it is difficult to find the right persons of any race for some of our vacancies. . . . I hope that all of us who represent theological education will step up our efforts to secure more Negroes as students to be trained both for the pastoral ministry and for theological teaching."[1] Later, the Rev. Dr. Lawrence N. Jones of Fisk, at Nashville, was named associate professor and dean of students at Union, to take up his duties February 1, 1965.

What is the situation elsewhere? Are good jobs within the churches open to Negroes in greater numbers than jobs outside the churches? The last few years have brought an increasing number of appointments of Negroes at various levels of church and missionary activity despite the fact that all church organizations face the same difficulty in finding qualified persons that Dr. Bennett cited in regard to Union.

In the churches too there are "firsts." In 1961, the Rev. Woodie W. White became the first Negro to be appointed associate pastor of a white Methodist church in Detroit. Another Methodist and Negro, the Rev. Wilbur R. Johnson, reported recently that his first year as pastor of a Tucson congregation gave "every evidence of complete acceptance." Mrs. Daisy H. Stocking, who had long headed a children's home at Daytona Beach, Florida, in 1964 was honored as the first Negro named to the Methodist Hall of Fame. Miss Emily Gibbes in 1959 was named executive secretary of the Women's Department of the United Presbyterian Board of Christian Education to direct the program of 800,000 women.

Methodist Bishop James K. Thomas became head of the predominantly white Iowa area in 1964; and one of the top

[1] From a letter to the editor.

administrative posts of the National Council of Churches, director of the Office of Public Interpretation, went to Samuel Proctor. The enumeration of such posts is not comprehensive—the list could be much longer—but we hope enough of a trend has been indicated to answer critics who say that church administration is lily-white.

Negroes have also been winning church elections. Back in 1958, the Rev. Dr. Gardner Calvin Taylor, pastor of a large interracial Baptist church in Brooklyn, was chosen president of the Protestant Council of the City of New York; he was both the first Negro and the youngest to get this position guiding 1,700 churches of 31 denominations. The New York State Baptist Convention elected the wife of a Syracuse Baptist pastor, Mrs. Leo R. Murphy, its first Negro president. In 1964, the Dallas Pastors Association in Texas named as president the Rev. Zan Wesley Holmes Jr., of Hamilton Park Methodist Church. Let it be admitted that there may be a bit of "tokenism" in this, but it is still significant.

Roman Catholicism marked a significant first in 1960. Cardinal Rugambwa, a Tanganyikan bishop, was named the first Negro cardinal that year and the next he became the first to preside at a mass in St. Patrick's Cathedral, New York. Of the 57,500 Roman Catholic priests in the United States, 115 are Negroes. (According to a survey published recently by the Catholic magazine, *The Sign,* most of the eighty-one Negro priests replying felt that the church was not giving adequate leadership on integration; but none was bitter, all rated their acceptance by white Catholics between "favorable" and "enthusiastic.") The Anglican Communion, which has two Negro prelates in Liberia, elected its first Negro suffragen bishop over white Episcopalian congregations in the United States; he was the Venerable John M. Burgess, archdeacon of Boston and one-time canon of Washington Cathedral—son of a dining car waiter. Said the new bishop: "The great advance made in race relations is miraculous, but of all institutions the church has been the least able to adjust to the change in racial atmosphere."

At the Episcopal general convention in the fall of 1964, the clergy voted overwhelmingly to approve civil disobedience when practiced "for reasons of conscience." But lay delegates in the House of Deputies rejected it two to one. Federal Judge Thurgood Marshall, the first Negro to represent New York, walked out in angry protest.

Two Protestant groups have had special problems this decade in integrating their organizations—the Methodists and the Presbyterians.

Since the 370,000 Negroes who are members of the Methodist Church equal the number who belong to all other Protestant bodies combined (aside from "Negro churches"), this denomination has had a particular problem in integration. Most of its Negroes have been organized in the Central Jurisdiction; for years Methodists worried about this outright segregation, but finally at the Quadrennial General Conference in Pittsburgh in 1964, a climax was reached.

A commission studying the question proposed that the Negro "conferences" be transferred into the "white" geographic jurisdictions in four years and that, if this does not move along satisfactorily, outright abolition would be proposed at the next Quadrennial in 1968. Opponents assailed this as gradualism close to a pattern already accepted in 1960. A Malaysian pastor said that overseas delegates would return home "discouraged and embarrassed" by this "plan of inaction." Pickets calling themselves "Methodists for Church Renewal" held an all-night prayer vigil, and in another protest about 1,000 demonstrators knelt at the entrance. But the commission plan was approved overwhelmingly.

Some observers felt the church had compromised too much. The Negro comedian Dick Gregory quipped: "When the church can hold its national convention and vote segregation in for four years, the Ku Klux Klan have to be able to OK it for another fifty."

Whether the Methodist compromise represents failure or statesmanlike wisdom will not be known for months. In the East action started immediately. A month after the Pittsburgh action, an area was established with 591 churches of New York City and vicinity; eight Negro churches from the Central Jurisdiction were transferred to it. A Negro minister was named superintendent of fifty-seven churches in Manhattan and the Bronx, and another became mission superintendent. Meantime, a new episcopal area was created in New Jersey. Twenty-one predominantly Negro churches were among the 600 admitted to it, and the Rev. Prince A. Taylor Jr. was named the first Negro to administer a predominantly white area; the annual conferences of Delaware and Washington, formerly headed by Bishop Taylor, were accepted into the Northeastern Jurisdictional Conference. "I think Negro Methodists are taking advantage of the opportunities for integration already," said Bishop Taylor, "but I think my appointment may make it more natural for them."

The Pittsburgh Quadrennial took several other significant actions on race: (1) elected a Negro president-designate; (2) voted to raise money to aid members suffering jail or deprivation because of race stands; (3) backed civil disobedience; (4) expressed willingness to discuss merger with three Negro Methodist denominations.

In recent years both Northern and Southern Presbyterians have taken steps toward integration at various levels.

The Rev. C. Lincoln McGee of Montclair became the first Negro to be moderator of the Presbytery of Newark, New Jersey, in 1958.[2] The Rev. W. Eugene Houston, a New York minister, later became the first Negro moderator of the New York State Synod.

The Rev. Lawrence W. Bottoms, a Louisville minister, was elected moderator of the Kentucky Synod of the Presbyterian, U. S. (Southern) denomination in 1962. The next year, the Rev. George Benjamin Brooks similarly became a "first"—moderator of the predominantly white presbytery at Phoenix, Arizona. In spite of Virginia's thorny racial problems, one of the state's presbyteries with 24,000 members, mostly white, elected a Negro moderator, the Rev. Irvin Elligan. In 1964, a Negro minister was named moderator of another Southern and predominantly white presbytery, at Mecklenburg, North Carolina.

Negroes or whites with liberal views on race also moved into the top positions of both these denominations at the national level.

In April, 1964, the Presbyterians, U. S., elected a liberal as moderator. The Rev. Felix B. Gear, a dean of Columbia Seminary in Georgia, beat a candidate of the conservative bloc 282 to 162. Dr. Gear said he "would not object" to ministers' participating in civil rights demonstrations and declared the church "should and will" get rid of its all-Negro presbyteries.

The denomination has had a segregation problem similar to that of the Methodists but on a smaller scale. A few thousand of its 937,000 members are in all-Negro presbyteries of the Deep South. But a few days after Dr. Gear's election, moving more rapidly than the Methodists, the

[2] When the Rev. Dr. Benjamin F. Glasco died at 82 in 1964, it was recalled that he had been elected first Negro moderator of the Presbytery of Philadelphia, in 1953.

Presbyterians in their General Assembly overrode the conservatives and instructed lower bodies to disband the segregated presbyteries and integrate them with white ones. The assembly also took a step to forbid exclusion of Negroes from any public worship in its churches.

A month later, the United Presbyterian, U. S. A. (Northern) General Assembly took an historic step at Oklahoma City.

Some years before, the Presbytery of New York had nominated as moderator of the national body a Negro minister, the Rev. Edler G. Hawkins, who already was this presbytery's moderator. By a close vote of 471 to 469, Dr. Hawkins was defeated. The defeat was no victory for conservatism, however, for the winner was the Rev. Herman Lee Turner, minister of the only "Northern" Presbyterian church in Atlanta, Georgia. He was a leading advocate of the "Atlanta Manifesto," in which ministers urged communication between Negroes and whites.

As national tensions rose in 1964, Dr. Hawkins became a nominee again. Dr. Houston (the New York Synod moderator mentioned above) told his Harlem congregation that "white backlash" might destroy any Negro's chance of winning. But he proved too pessimistic. Dr. Hawkins won, 465 to 368, and so became the first Negro chief of 3.2 million United Presbyterians, most of them white.

Dr. Hawkins' election at fifty-five climaxed a career of long vigor in interracial activity. Shortly after he left Union Theological Seminary, he went to a small Bronx church that had been abandoned by white members, leaving only nine Negro parishioners. Under him it grew to be a multiracial, multilingual body of more than a thousand. He served two one-year terms as head of the 120 churches of the New York Presbytery and then was secretary of the national church's Commission on Race and Religion.

At Oklahoma City, however, another Negro minister sounded a word of caution. He was the Rev. Eugene S. Callender, pastor of a Harlem church and a successor of Dr. Hawkins as New York moderator.

"Let us not point too quickly with pride," he suggested. "Let us remember that as long as we have segregated homes for the aged, as long as we maintain in our investment portfolios stocks of industries that do not have fair employment practices—we continue to be wrong in the sight of God.

"As long as white Presbyterians continue to move out of their neighborhoods when Negroes move in, as long as we continue to support backward local school boards in our local communities, we are wrong."

10 · Why a "Negro Church"?

If half the amount of churches that have been
burned down in Mississippi in the last two weeks had
been burned down in Moscow, Russia, it would be on
every front page of the papers in America, and we
would be upset about it. And when you get upset
about what happens in Russia and you can't get upset
about what happens in America, you're in trouble. You
are in trouble.

—Dick Gregory

When Reinhold Niebuhr was a young minister in
Detroit in the twenties, the automobile industry attracted
many Negroes to the area. The man who was to become a
famous Protestant theologian was named chairman of a
city committee on race relations, and four Negro families
began to come to his church regularly. They were professional people, and the church, he found, was "proud to
have them."

But the Negroes maintained responsible positions in
their own Negro churches. Niebuhr took up with his official
board the question of possible membership. The board
approved, but neither the families nor their churches wanted
them to make the shift.

More than a generation has passed, but much the same
thing could happen today. Some Negroes venture out into

inclusive churches. But most Negroes—an estimated ten million—go to segregated churches for very much the same reason that their children are enrolled in segregated schools.

Their churches are close to home. Negroes are either not welcomed warmly in some so-called white churches or they are actually barred. But even where the white church is close and friendly, the Negro Christian may feel most at home in the denomination or congregation he has long been familiar with.

I have belonged during various periods of my life and in various cities to both white and Negro churches. There have been cities where a white church apealed to me most because of the greater opportunity it presented for Christian witness and service. Usually this was in a city or town with a small Negro population.

But when Negroes are gathered together in His name— even if there are only a few of them—there is a quality of spirit in the worship and witness that is missing in most white middle-class churches. In the latter the membership seems to have lost its faith in and dependency on God. He has become for them a very silent partner to whom they feel they need never turn because they've learned to handle all their own problems. They remind me of the prosperous and self-satisfied farmer whose pastor remarked that the Lord and he had certainly done wonders with the farm. The farmer replied: "Yes, but you should have seen it when the Lord had it by himself!"

Today, during the civil rights struggle, belonging to a white church is out of the question for me. The ministers do a great job of speaking out against injustice. They go on Freedom Rides, they demonstrate, they even go to jail. But the members! If any large number of them followed their pastors' leadership, more of us Negroes would be living in decent houses and have better jobs.

The Negro church is part of me—my heritage. When the minister calls on a partially blind sister to lead us in prayer, and majestic, humble, figurative words pour from her soul, I believe that they travel by the most direct line to the mercy seat of God. When the choir sings, "City Called Heaven," or a soloist baritones, "Sometimes I Feel Like a Motherless Child," I am proud of and thankful for the courage of my ancestors. I am aware once more that we Negroes have indeed "come to the place for which our fathers sighed."

There is also the question of status. The ordinary layman can have both position and confidence in his Negro church that he would not gain so readily in an integrated one, at least for a time. And the clergyman has power and authority in his denomination and local parish that are not easily relinquished; for example, though the Methodist Church with its Central Jurisdiction has a membership of only 4 percent Negroes, one in nine active U.S. Methodist bishops is a Negro. What happens to the Negro Methodist minister or Negro layman in, say, Alabama, if they are absorbed into white conferences?

The Negro church is many things. In parts of the South it is a martyr church. Between June 15 and August 15, 1964, fifteen Negro churches in Mississippi were burned—almost two a week! The AP put the total at thirty-four in November. Most of such burnings in recent years have been, ironically, in the "Bible Belt."

It used to be that churches were considered sacred in the South, but as the rights movement began to gain momentum several years ago, the burnings began. At Sasser, Georgia, for example, three Negro churches were burned in 1962. They were rebuilt with contributions of more than $100,000 raised throughout the nation. But burnings and bombings went on.

"I am pastor of four congregations in Adams County," said the Rev. Shead Baldwin as he stared at the ashes of a church burned at Natchez on a July Sunday dawn. "One of my other churches was burned the same way eleven months ago. It is still to be rebuilt."

Since some church buildings are used for civil rights meetings, the unarrested arsonists no doubt would argue that the structures are no longer sacred. But the Adams churches had not been used for meetings, and Mr. Baldwin said that, while he had once voted, he had been barred from the polls for years.

"I guess it's just something to try to frighten people," he said in bewilderment.

Twenty-three Mississippi churchmen, representing Roman Catholics, Protestants and Jews, formed an interracial Committee of Concern to help with reconstruction of the burned churches. Included are three bishops—a Methodist, an Episcopalian and a Catholic.

In the North, independent storefront churches have proliferated to help give Negroes strength and identity—our middle-sized city has sixteen. These understanding, enthusiastic bands of believers, in the words of one student, Ira E. Harrison, are brought by preachers "toward a state of sanctification which helps to keep them from 'hurt, harm, and danger.'"

Negro churches provide social as well as religious leadership. In Philadelphia, Negro Methodists and Baptists worked with a first Negro judge, Raymond Pace Alexander, to create an auxiliary probation system for Negro criminals. A Methodist Negro church in Dallas completed a housing project for 172 families. A Baptist church in Brooklyn started a restaurant and supermarket recently to provide jobs for Negroes. After the Harlem riots, thirty-five Negro churches of nine Protestant denominations held an outdoor rally to witness against hooliganism. Negro churches in California even sent a white missionary—said to be the first so commissioned—to work in Asia.

But in recent years the major contribution of the Negro church has been the gift of voices. More and more in the North, Negro pastors are stepping outside their parishes to speak as prophets on the race issue. And in the South, the Negro church has given its leaders—Martin Luther King Jr., Ralph D. Abernathy and many unsung pastors—to the nonviolent revolution. It is hardly too much to say that, without the dynamic provided from the Negro churches, the American civil rights movement would have been stalled on dead center in the last decade.

As in the young Niebuhr's time, Negroes do not flock from their churches to join inclusive ones. It must be admitted that a factor in this may be that integration of the churches is usually thought of as admitting Negroes to "white" churches. White Christians should also consider joining Negro congregations. The Episcopal Society for Cultural and Racial Unity, which lists three bishops on its board, recently said: "For too long we have expected the Negro alone to take the initiative. Now let white Christians demonstrate their commitment by joining in the minority status with Negro churchmen. Neither may say he has no need of the other."

Not everything is perfect in the Negro church. Sometimes the paint is peeling. Hymn books are often old and in short supply. The art work, stained glass, organ and furnishings cannot compare with those in most white churches. Announcements are not always handled with finesse. And the quality of worship is marred in some Negro churches where the words and melodies of great hymns and spirituals are drowned by a new double-clapping and boogie-beat. But while these factors hinder the worship for me, I am nevertheless conscious of a pervading atmosphere of fervor.

When the struggle is over, and Negro Christians and white Christians merge into Christian Christians, I hope that the Negroes bring along this spirituality as their contribution.

11 · The "Southern Church" and the "Northern Church"

> In the South as well as in the North more bars are open to Negroes than churches and more cinemas than schools. What good is . . . a religion which keeps him outside its church?
>
> —Dr. Dagobert Runes

The Associated Press told the story starkly to the whole world from Augusta, Georgia:

Two Negro students, one a Baptist minister, tried unsuccessfully to worship in two Augusta white churches.

The Rev. Roosevelt Green Jr., 21 years old, and Paul Thompkins, 22, students at Paine College, first tried to enter the First Baptist Church. An usher denied them admittance, and they left without an argument.

Crossing the street, Mr. Green and Mr. Thompkins sought to enter St. John's Methodist Church. Again they were rebuffed when the door was barred and church officials waved them on. The students stood quietly outside at the foot of the church steps and about fifty persons gathered. Some parishioners entering the church made unfriendly remarks, others ignored the Negroes.

After about fifteen minutes, Marion Dasher, chairman of the church board, told the Negroes:

"You are not welcome at this church."[1]

[1] The story appeared in newspapers on November 26, 1961.

What a long way the church had come since Paul sweated on long journeys through Asia Minor to find people who would listen to the gospel! Once there was no room for the Christ child in the inn; today there is sometimes no room for him in the church!

The incident in Georgia, during November of 1961, was only one of many that fall. The "kneel-in" movement had begun in August that year when a small band of Negro students entered an all-white church in Atlanta to worship with fellow-Christians. During the next six months, it was reported, at least 200 similar demonstrations took place around the nation. In Jackson, Mississippi, at Eastertide in 1964, a Methodist church even turned away two Methodist bishops because one of them was Negro!

An international dimension of segregation is indicated by these words written to a university chaplain by a woman teacher from India, a political science Ph.D., who was seized when she tried to attend a Jackson Methodist church with two Negroes and a white dean:

I was infuriated, stunned, shocked and rudely awakened to the brutalities of these people. I told the person who was holding my arms, "I am from India. If you want you can see my passport."

There was no answer. The strong hand of the man pushed me with all its force.

I refuse to accept that a well-dressed man in the United States in 1964 could use his physical force against a woman, a woman from a foreign land, in front of the church. . . .

Sometimes kneel-inners have simply been barred; at other times arrests have resulted. Three Negroes who tried to attend Sunday services at the First Baptist Church in Albany, Georgia, were arrested, and integrated kneel-in groups were turned away from six other churches there.

But bewilderment appears to be the typical reaction of

the Southern Christian. Why would Negroes want to go to a white church? Mississippi Methodists at the 1964 Quadrennial presented the argument that kneel-in Christians were not sincere but were seeking publicity. This raises the question of whether the church insists on sincerity and sinlessness in a potential convert before opening the Bible to him. One wonders how the conservative Christian can look forward to the Judgment Day with anything less than anguish if he has kept someone he considers a sinning soul from hearing the Word. Surely this is a sin much more heinous than the thefts and lies that he believes merit punishment. And what are the prospects on Judgment Day of arsonists —some of them no doubt "Christians"—who burn Negro houses of worship?

In the summer of 1964, a group of white teen-agers from a Pennsylvania Presbyterian church went to Elm City, North Carolina, planning to paint a rural Negro church and open a Bible school, one of hundreds of such Presbyterian service programs. A tense situation arose, and the Ku Klux Klan threatened them, forcing them to leave.

Elo L. Henderson, a representative of the church's all-Negro Catawba Synod, asked for older volunteers. "The time has come," he said, "for our church to make a decision regarding the South, that the full resources of the Board of National Missions will be behind any national missions project which may be similarly threatened or endangered."

So seventeen white and Negro volunteers went in. The Klan threatened they would "never lay a brush" on the church. But they stayed at integrated motels nearby and began painting. The grand dragon of the North Carolina Klan twice appeared at the church to warn against an integrated project. Then early one morning, two young men poured gas on the church steps and were about to light it when a deputy sheriff fired warning shots and arrested them. Highway patrolmen moved in to stand guard, and in four days the volunteers finished the painting.

Meantime, the vacation Bible school was started for about forty Negro pupils. Teaching them were six Negro and white ministers.

The charge of communism, time-worn as it is, is still repeated against churchmen who want interracial brotherhood, and this arson of the tongue can be even more dangerous than church-burning in destroying careers and livings. More than five years ago, social action leaders of seven Protestant denominations warned of a "Southern version of McCarthyism" that was attempting to silence ministers.

Amid such slanders, burnings, threats and rejections of Negroes at church doors, the work of making the Christian church color-blind in the South goes on. One of the most difficult careers today is being a Southern minister. Yet many ministers work unobtrusively to try to change attitudes. Sometimes they risk being charged as conspirators by meeting together, as if in the catacombs. Thurgood Marshall, then chief counsel of the NAACP, has said there was "at least one committee of white clergymen in every state in the South" working for integration. This clerical underground has been reported to have 6 or 8 members in Mississippi and about 160 in Alabama.

Tragically, however, "silence" is the word that best characterizes the segregated church in most of the South. One reads in the newspapers of ushers who tell Negroes they can't enter a church, but one looks in vain for the stories of a minister or congregational leader who repudiates the ushers' rudeness or even speaks a friendly word to the Negroes kept outside. In *The Christian Century*, Samuel Southard of Louisville, Kentucky, pointed out that the Southern Baptist Mission Board has printed articles against segregation, but nothing is said about the fact that the same convention deletes references to Negroes from Sunday school publications. "Some denominational officials," he wrote, "are apparently united in a conspiracy of silence with pastors who uphold the political and social status quo. The ecclesiastical screen of silence has been most successfully broken by missionaries and by one evangelist, Billy Graham."[2]

At Eastertime, 1964, Billy Graham spoke to 35,000 persons in Birmingham, the largest integrated audience ever assembled in Alabama; he hammered at prejudice, and a Negro minister offered prayer. Long before, at the time of the Little Rock crisis, Graham had held an integrated meeting there. "The best way to start loving a man," he says, "is to pray for him."

"Silent White Ministers of the South" was the title of a *New York Times Magazine* article by George McMillan, a writer of Aiken, South Carolina. "Some ministers, of course, have spoken up courageously, even at the cost of their pulpits," he said, ". . . but the great majority of the estimated 50,000 white Southern clergymen continue to stand silent about racial matters. They stand silent in the face of racial incidents across the country."[3]

Another *Christian Century* writer, Alfred Klausler, reported that a white minister told him that the question of school integration is "never broached" by either ministers or laymen in any church group of Prince Edward County, Virginia. But he quotes a Negro Baptist, the Rev. L. Francis Griffin, president of the Prince Edward County Christian Association:

[2] Excerpt from Reader's Response "Self-Criticism in the South," by Samuel Southard. Copyright 1962 Christian Century Foundation. Reprinted by permission from the December 5 issue of *The Christian Century*.

[3] *The New York Times Magazine*, April 5, 1964.

The clergy and their communicants are the most hardened of all about this situation [school segregation]. The majority of the ministers and their people fail to realize that there is any moral issue involved in this tragedy. They regard me and my fellow workers as troublemakers . . . . The prophetic voice is totally lacking among the white Protestant clergy . . . . I believe the white ministers are dictated to by the pews . . . . Somewhere, somehow, my white brethren must be given courage to become prophets.[4]

In another *New York Times Magazine* article, a Southern white minister virtually pleaded guilty to charges of silence. As a young minister in Texas, said the Rev. Robert Collie, now a preacher in the small Louisiana town of Kentwood, he had spoken out against segregation, but his people merely complained that he had used the privilege of the pulpit when they couldn't talk back. And did anyone really believe ministers' preaching changed attitudes?

"There is, of course, the power of personal persuasion, and I and most other ministers do not take full advantage of this opportunity," he conceded. "But if I, for instance, differ sufficiently and strongly enough with my congregation to tell them they are all headed for hell if they don't change their value structure, they being Americans, are the kind of people who will reply that if I am so keen on the place, I can go there myself."[5]

The comment, of course, demonstrates the decline in the potency of the concept of sin and hell. Neither ministers nor parishioners believe they will go to hell if they sin against the Negro; and they lack imagination about the hell on earth that can result from continued condescension and insult toward the colored peoples of the world. Yet

[4] "The Shame and the Glory," by Alfred Klausler, in *The Christian Century*, August 15, 1962, pp. 977-979.

[5] "A 'Silent Minister' Speaks Up," by Robert Collie, in *The New York Times Magazine*, May 24, 1964, pp. 12f.

there are hints of change. In the same article in which he deplored silence, for example, Mr. McMillan told of his surprise that the minister of youth in a Columbia church, the largest Baptist one in South Carolina, testified in the capitol for desegregation of state parks. So he went to see the senior minister, the Rev. Archie Ellis.

"You were surpised to see Roger down there at the Capitol?" Mr. Ellis asked. "Well, that's all right. Nothing's going to happen to him. Things have changed, you know. You have got to realize that this thing is before people daily now. There is a turn-about of thinking. I can refer to this thing now without any great resistance on the part of my congregation."

In apparent reference to a Negro, he said one had worshiped in church on Sunday and he himself had not even known it until Wednesday. And he added:

"The time has come when the clergy can do a great deal through a quiet, unsensational approach to the key people in this area."

This type of quiet talking appears to be one of the most fruitful approaches in the South during the sixties. On the defensive, fearful that any militance will only stir violent opposition, Southern churchmen may find that keeping discussion alive is as radical as they can get for awhile.

Some years ago, Brooks Hays, the Arkansas Congressman, was beaten by a write-in vote for a segregationist. A few months later, retiring as president of the Southern Baptist Convention, he urged that white and Negro church leaders of the South carry on talks as "a practical step" toward solving race problems.

Later, a group of white clergymen in racked Birmingham sounded the same note. They pledged themselves publicly to "make efforts to re-establish better communications between the races."

The executive committee of the Episcopal Diocese of Mississippi urged citizens to keep lines of communication open "in a spirit of Christian understanding." The mayor of Mobile, Alabama, which has been generally tranquil, has said: "The chief element in the formula is communications. Local Negro leaders know they can come here and get a fair hearing for their grievances."

This idea of talking between the races is also a major objective of the civil rights movement, even of demonstrations. Many whites feel that it is better for people to talk together than kill each other. Others regard Negroes at home as they do Red Chinese abroad: they should be ignored and excluded, and any suggestion of sitting down with them is subversive. One of the least things American Christians can do is keep the channels of communication open between churchmen of our two big race blocs.

The place was a small college town in Kentucky; the time was fall; students from America and all parts of the world were arriving. One member of this group was . . . an African . . . . He had come under the influence of Baptist missionaries and had been able to come to America to pursue his studies. Already he was a distinguished scholar in English literature, spoke several languages, and was in constant demand for discussion groups and religious services. His religious conviction and knowledge of the Bible, coupled with his charm, impressed both students and faculty.

The fateful day occurred the first Sunday on campus. My friend had naturally decided to attend the local Baptist church, since, through being a part of the larger Baptist organization, it had contributed so much to his development. I attended another and it was only that evening that I got the full story from him. I don't know whether anyone gave him any warning of what to expect; certainly he was acutely unprepared and shocked, as were his white-skinned fellow students, when after the service he was called aside by several of the church deacons. "It would be better if you didn't come back to this church," was the way one of them put it. "You can worship at the church on the campus."

My friend's shame and humiliation were immeasurable. "Never before have I been subjected to such a degrading experience," he said to me in his room that night. We talked about the hypocrisy and incomprehensibility of a church that sends missionaries and then acts so inanely toward one of its converts . . . .

There were repercussions from this incident. The Baptist group of youths fell to be a handful; one of the church's youth directors who seemed to feel that something was wrong in the church was fired; and, of course, the deacons saw to it that they weren't caught napping again by the brazen entrance of a Negro youth who went into their church as if he belonged there. And I will never forget that look in his eye . . . .[6]

This story about a 1952 incident in a border state, recalled in a letter to the *Saturday Review* by Peter R. Whitis, a California doctor, requires no elaboration. The church simply has to confront the irony and hypocrisy of such an account. Missionaries, unwilling to renounce their life's dedication, have sometimes helped break through even to reactionaries. In the Presbyterian, U. S., denomination, 202 missionaries signed a 1964 appeal saying "our witness is affected adversely" by "various forms of racial segregation in the church." Josephine Scaggs, a Southern Baptist missionary in Nigeria, critized American church women who had declined when she offered to bring a Nigerian convert to their mission meetings—they were honoring Africa in their hearts, she said, but not their homes. One young man who was active in the New Orleans sit-ins explained he was the son of Southern Baptist missionaries, and he had grown up without prejudice. Mr. Southard, in the article quoted above, argued that "self-criticism by Southerners may sometimes stem from missionary motives":

[6] A Letter to the Editor, by Peter R. Whitis in *Saturday Review*, July 4, 1964, p. 15.

John Claypool paved the way toward integration of Crescent Hill Baptist Church in Louisville by welcoming from the pulpit a Nigerian couple who were converted under Southern Baptist missions . . . . Missionary-minded faculty members at Georgetown College in Kentucky led the Georgetown Baptist Church to admit two Nigerian students as members. Leo Eddleman, the president under whom Georgetown College admitted Negro students, was formerly a missionary in Israel.[7]

When Dr. Eddleman became president of New Orleans Baptist Seminary, he employed a seminary student who had lost his job as a result of keeping his child in a desegregating school.

In the summer of 1964 the Southern Baptists made an important advance when their convention sponsored two conferences dealing with race. "Our attitude towards people of other races," warned one leader, "is definitely curbing our evangelistic outreach, both at home and around the world."

The Christian churches' inconsistency and hypocrisy have been an Achilles heel. Some young liberal intellectuals have left to make the civil rights movement their religion rather than try to reform the church, and Protestantism's own leaders have denounced her shortcomings repeatedly. Not long ago, preaching to an overflow crowd at New York City's huge Riverside Church, Dr. Martin Luther King Jr. cried: "Millions of American Negroes have knocked again and again on the doors of so-called white churches, but they have usually been greeted by a cold indifference or a blatant hypocrisy."

How many church members know that Malcolm X, the late Negro leader who turned to a form of Islam, grew up as a Christian but said he turned from the church be-

---

[7] Except from Reader's Response "Self-Criticism in the South," by Samuel Southard. Copyright 1962, Christian Century Foundation. Reprinted by permission from the December 5 issue *The Christian Century*.

cause of its race hypocrisy? His father was a midwest Baptist minister. Twice their home was burned down while Malcolm was a boy, once in Nebraska, once in Michigan. "It was Christians who burned the home in both places— people who teach, you know, religious tolerance and brotherhood," he said. And he added bitterly: "Even before I went to prison, I had already become an atheist and I could see the hypocrisy of Christianity. Most of my associates were white; they were either Jews or Christians, and I saw hypocrisy on both sides. None of them really practiced what they preached."

One of the big motive powers in integrating churches has been to do away with this hypocrisy. At the head of ten proposals for church action, the General Assembly of the National Council of Churches in 1963 put the flat objective: "All Christian Churches should in fact be open to all regardless of race and should publicly so declare." In some areas, especially in the South, it is still news when a church integrates, but it does happen. By a three to two margin, the congregation of University Baptist Church in Chapel Hill, North Carolina, voted to integrate. A survey of Texas churches showed that two-thirds of those with more than 1,200 members have at least some degree of inclusiveness. In the North, where customs are more fluid, or at least more fuzzy and uncertain, wider experimentation in church integration has been possible, but success is neither easy nor automatic.

At Troy, New York, a Negro church and a white church joined hands—but after a struggle. The Negro church, Liberty Presbyterian, had been started about 1835 when First Presbyterian decided it would be better if the "colored help" stopped crowding the upstairs gallery. But urban renewal came to Troy in the 1960's. Liberty Church was given two years to move.

The Negro church was not strong. With only thirty families, it decided merger was the only way to go on, and if it were to remain Presbyterian, it would have to merge with a white church. A committee decided to sound out the Rev. Robert M. Marsano, pastor of Oakwood Presbyterian Church, uptown. He had "never given the integration problem much thought," but, feeling he had to favor the idea, he took it up with the twelve elders. Only four of them were strongly with him. Soon the tensions became so great that one of these had to resign because of the threat to his health.

Should Liberty members be invited to a get-acquainted service? The elders split, and the minister broke the tie by voting to hold the service. Some Oakwood parishioners walked out of the service just before he preached.

Then the Albany Presbytery got into it. An agreement was reached whereby Oakwood, without calling it merger, invited Liberty members to come to the church, and gave them official representation on church bodies. The first wave of sixteen Negro members arrived on an autumn Sunday, two days after the assassination of President Kennedy. Mr. Marsano had to change his sermon little because of the Dallas tragedy. "On this momentous occasion when we are confronting transition and change," he preached, "surely it is appropriate for us to reflect upon the meaning and implications of the promises we made when we united with the church."

Further groups of the Negroes joined, and new white members came to the church.

"I work with Negroes; I think they're nice people," said a nurse's aide, one of the newcomers. But others were not so open-minded. Five elders and 10 percent of the whites left the church. Income dropped 35 percent. Money from sale of the Negro church helped the budget problem, however. Whites continued to come in, so net membership grew from 280 to 350. One person said he joined because this was a church that practiced what it preached. He was a Troy newspaperman who had come to write about the scrap!

One metallurgist, an elder, favored the move strongly: "The reason the church has become an anemic institution is that it has not involved itself with the issues of its time. Too often churches are allowed to become select little clubs."

Significantly, the church's young people backed up the merger. "It was shameful and disgraceful," said one of them, speaking of the dissension, "that a group of Christians should act this way."

Many other stories of the integration of Northern churches in the last half dozen years could be added, but a number of accounts of the first wave of such efforts were given in *Progress Against Prejudice* and the list need not be extended here.

However, the story of one midwest church should be told because of several unusual aspects.

The Mennonite Church, with a number of small wings, is thought of by most Americans who know it slightly as related to old Germany, to prosperous "Pennsylvania Dutch" farms. But the stereotype is shattered in Lee Heights, southeast of Cleveland, Ohio.

The Community Church there is a mission church started in a grade school. Only two persons came to the first service in 1957, but the pastor, Vern Miller, labored on, and membership has gone well past a hundred. Lee Heights is unusual in being an interracial suburb, and the congregation is thoroughly integrated, at all levels. While the Sunday School superintendent is white, the clerk is a Negro. And a Negro woman teaches an integrated class dressed in

Mennonite tradition with a little white cap on the back of her head.

Spiritual vitality is cited as the cause for the growth of this church. This was the emphasis of the sign on its former barracks-like building:

GLADSTONE MENNONITE CHURCH
Biblical   Interracial   Evangelical

The success of this church, overcoming the gaps among old-world customs and racial differences and middle-class impulses in a fast growing suburb, should help quench the timidity of those fearful to attempt integration under much more optimistic circumstances.

For the sake of objectivity, we might look to another area of the world where American liberties and American traditions are not involved. South Africa has an apartheid policy that separates the races as callously as any nation on the globe, and the Presbyterian Church in South Africa is considered one of the most conservative Protestant denominations in regard to race. Yet here is a story of change even there.

In the spring of 1962, the Presbyterian congregation at East London began an experiment in multiracial worship. The group met every Sunday evening; about half were whites and the other half Africans and "coloreds." Reporting to the church's general assembly at Capetown some months later, the Rev. J. D. Robertson said that the mixing has been "genuine and happy."

"The atmosphere was alive, hopeful, and noticeably devoid of racial tension," he said. "The races mixed without artificiality, reserve or forwardness."

What a conservative church in South Africa can do, American churches ought to be willing to attempt!

12 · Leaven Within Leaven

> Except for pioneering leaders in some denominations and courageous ministers and laymen scattered here and there, the mass of white Christians is confused and immobilized by the immensity of the nation's racial crisis.
>
> —Kyle Haselden

Twenty-eight young white Methodist ministers in Mississippi issued a manifesto in 1963, proclaiming belief in "freedom of the pulpit" and opposing discrimination in the state where they were born. Immediately, all of them were subjected to boycotts and other harassment by their congregations, and most had to leave the state.

Firings of pastors have occurred in both North and South. An official of the National Council of Churches recently said that sixty white ministers had lost their jobs because of activity related to the race issue during just the preceding six months.

In Cairo, Illinois, a Presbyterian church soloist who owns a restaurant put a padlock on the door to close it to Negroes (other patrons were let in the back door). The deacon of a white church in the community said: "Niggers are not welcome here."

That sentiment, if unspoken, is the sentiment of many

white Protestant churchmen, possibly most. Pollster Sam Lubell found in 1961 interviews in the South that "only four of every ten thought Negroes should worship in the same churches" as whites. A Dallas woman said: "I'd let them into our churches, because those are God's houses, but I wouldn't want them at church socials or in my house." A 1961 survey by the Boston University School of Theology indicated that three out of ten Methodists do· not favor desegregation; only about half of them believe in equal opportunity! A Harvard psychologist summarized several studies: "On the average, churchgoers and professedly religious people have considerably more prejudice than do non-churchgoers and non-believers."

Nevertheless, temporal leaders look to the churches to awaken the conscience of America. Burke Marshall, the chief civil rights official in the Justice Department, has said that the churches have not sufficiently emphasized the moral aspects of segregation: "I think the churches in general have not shown enough leadership in educating the people in the North as well as in the South on that subject." When 150 Southern Baptist leaders visited the rose garden at the White House in the spring of 1964, President Johnson called on them to be "prophets in our time" who would help "build a house of freedom where all men can dwell." A month later he called on 177 visiting leaders of Protestant, Roman Catholic and Jewish groups to "direct the immense power of religion" to bring racial brotherhood. "Stir our consciences," he pleaded. At the end of his "sermon" in the East Room, someone said, "Amen."

Of course some churchmen have spoken courageously. The *Interracial News Service* of the National Council of Churches published portions of major church statements made for interracial brotherhood between 1961 and 1963, and they filled twelve finely-printed pages. Denominations represented were Armenian, American Baptist, Seventh Day Baptist, Southern Baptist, Brethren, Disciples of Christ, Friends, Greek Orthodox, Lutheran, African Methodist Episcopal Zion, Christian Methodist Episcopal, Methodist, Moravian, Presbyterian, U.S., United Presbyterian, U.S.A., Protestant Episcopal, Reformed, Syrian Antiochian Orthodox, Unitarian Universalist, and United Church of Christ. The World Council of Churches, which spoke for racial brotherhood at Evanston in 1954, has reiterated its condemnation of racial segregation as contrary to the Gospels. In one of the sharpest and most recent of race statements the Lutheran Church in America, speaking out in the summer of 1964 in favor of peaceful demonstrations when laws and customs conflict with "the moral law of God," significantly added:

"If and when the means of legal recourse have been exhausted or have been demonstrably inadequate, Christians may then choose to serve the cause of racial justice by disobeying a law that clearly involves the violation of their obligations as Christians."

Roman Catholicism has fought racism with both words and action. In a widely-publicized case, the Archbishop of New Orleans excommunicated three segregationists who had attempted to arouse opposition to the desegregation of church schools. A leader of the National Catholic Welfare Conference has called on Catholics, in brotherhood, to "meet socially, and this includes visiting homes."

One of the major developments of the sixties, in the wake of the wider ecumenicity spurred by Pope John, has been the beginning of interfaith cooperation in removing racial barriers. Catholics, Protestants, Jews and Orthodox joined in early 1963 in a National Conference on Religion and Race and sizable grants of money were given, chiefly by the National Catholic Welfare Conference and the National Council of Churches for an eighteen-month program of publishing conference findings, evaluating accomplishments of the meeting, and proposing further joint program ideas to the participating groups. As a result of the meeting and follow-up, many local communities organized their own inter-religious committees to implement the findings of the conference with action programs.

Churches have also backed up their words with hard cash. As far back as 1959, the Congregational Christian Churches and the United Presbyterian Church in the U.S.A. voted to provide aid to churches that have suffered financially as a result of integration. Four years later the Presbyterians allocated half a million dollars to a special commission to fight racial discrimination. During 1964, the National Council's Commission on Religion and Race set up a Church Restoration Fund to channel money to churches damaged as a result of racial strife.

The United Church of Christ in 1963 (electing Mrs. Robert C. Johnson, a Negro woman from Birmingham, as assistant moderator) voted to try to raise a million for bail and legal costs for demonstrators, and to give financial help to members who lost their jobs because of civil rights activities.

What we have, in short, is a struggle within the church to lead to decency. Some Christians, with twisted logic, oppose brotherhood; many more are apathetic. But the world looks to the churches for moral leadership. A prophetic few, both clergy and laymen, dedicate their minds and voices and hours and dollars to bringing change. It is neither fair nor accurate to say that the churches have not cared. But not enough churchmen in enough churches have so far cared enough.

Words sometimes are dismissed as only talk; but there are times when words require courage and challenge men to change their minds. Here are a few of the more outspoken Christian comments from the South in recent years:

—The Rev. Dr. Herman L. Turner, the United Presbyterian moderator mentioned in Chapter 9, said members had been lost in his Georgia church because of a stand for integration, but added: "The church cannot stand on the firing line in this struggle without having casualties."

—The Rev. Duncan M. Gray Jr., an Episcopal rector in Oxford, Mississippi, called Gov. Ross R. Barnett "a living symbol of lawlessness" after the effort to bar a Negro student from the University of Mississippi.

—Dr. Howard M. Reaves, president of the Alabama Baptist Convention in 1962, commented when Gov. George C. Wallace asked for the prayers of convention delegates: "If and when the days of tension come to Alabama as they did a few weeks ago in Mississippi, we look to you as chief executive of the state to take a stand for law and order, irrespective of whether you agree with certain judicial decisions which may be handed down."

A 17-year-old girl in New Jersey had to take a stand when she found racism in conflict with her Christianity. Lynn Van Dyke, youth moderator of the Presbytery of Elizabeth, was elected leader of the Rainbow Girls there. She got into a jam simply because she wanted to invite to the installation a girl she had met on a National Missions Study Tour in Puerto Rico, a Negro. She was told not to. That made her decide to appoint a committee to study segregation in the girls' order, and a telegram came down from the supreme inspector that she should resign if she did not accept the rules she had taken on "as a Rainbow Christian Girl."

Lynn thought two days. Then, according to an account in *Presbyterian Life,* she gave an answer which was "not that of a Rainbow Christian Girl but a Christian Rainbow Girl." She replied that she had been elected by members who knew she would make an "effort to bring Rainbow rules into line with American and Christian conscience." So "as a Christian" she could not accept the order. She was expelled.[1]

Strong speech and strong actions are required, and still change comes slowly.

There are a number of different ways of bringing social progress, and churchmen have tried most of them in the race area. Since citizens disagree about which methods are effective and moral, a great deal of civil rights energy is often diverted into debate over method. There can never be general agreement. But analysis of three major approaches may give those who want change a better understanding of different roles in the struggle.

Agitation. The agitator tries to dramatize, perhaps in a shocking fashion, the revolutionary demand for an upset of values and behavior. He feels that the status quo is so bad that drastic means are necessary. The more moderate person worries lest the agitators' methods harm the whole movement. And the stand-patter dismisses the agitator as "a Communist."

Political Activity. The liberal citizen may turn to political action for new laws and administration, to improve the lot of minority groups. He will perhaps criticize the agitator for action he considers unrealistic and irrelevant, saying it does not come to grips with the power structure directly; and in turn he will be criticized as a compromiser and even a coward by the more radical activist. The conservative, on the other hand, will probably consider the liberal politician a precursor of anarchy; and the right-wing extremist will doubtless lump agitators and politicians together as a part of "the Communist conspiracy."

Education. Many believe that only change in the hearts of men by persuasion and education can ever eliminate racial friction. Agitators and liberal politicians would probably feel

[1] "Exchange of Telegrams," in *Presbyterian Life,* December 15, 1962.

that sole reliance on education may mean, at best, too little too late; at worst, it may cover indifference or the desire for delay. But the person who puts his whole trust in education typically feels that agitation and politics are inappropriate for the church and perhaps lacking in dignity. He may believe that action in the streets and legislative halls rouses fears and backlash.

Of course, the categories are not mutually exclusive. A person may combine work in agitation, politics and persuasion. And there are gradations. A political activist may, in his less compromising moods, join in a demonstration; and the minister who views his role as educator may be moved to help get out the votes for an issue he views as deeply moral.

So too there may be an unconscious teamwork among persons who represent the three categories. Without agitation, the people might never awake; without the hard compromises of political work, no part of the vision might ever be crystallized into practical reality. But without the firm base provided by educational activity, the work of pickets and lobbyists might be lost in a quicksand of misunderstanding and hate. More understanding of the different roles that are needed—more tolerance of the fact that conscience drives equally sincere people to struggle in different ways—would no doubt result in a more cooperative attack and therefore a much more effective struggle against racial indecencies.

At the level of agitation, ministers and laymen have joined in nonviolent direct action for integration. They have participated in bus boycotts and marches and sit-ins and kneel-ins and picketing, to overcome segregation both inside the church and outside. We have seen how Episcopal clergymen made a prayer pilgrimage to Mississippi; and the Presbyterian leader, Dr. Eugene Carson Blake, and other churchmen received nationwide coverage when they joined in a 1963 demonstration to integrate an amusement park in Maryland.

A still more dramatic stand was taken by the Rev. Clayton K. Hewett of an Episcopal church in Pennsylvania. He was arrested in a Chester demonstration and began an "indefinite fast" to protest racism in the city. He broke the hunger strike eighteen days later after the Governor's intervention gave him hope of progress at Chester.

One of the largest of all the demonstrations of religious leaders, aside from the March on Washington, was that which climaxed nine months of effort in 1962 to desegregate all public facilities in Albany, Georgia. Seventy-five clergymen and church members, men and women, young and old, took part. They marched two by two in front of the City Hall, stood in silence, then read a passage of Scripture and said a prayer. Police swarmed around and asked their purpose.

"We have come to offer prayers to God," said one of the demonstrators.

Then, sounding for all the world like the satrap of a distant pagan land being opened by missionaries, Police Chief Laurie Pritchett told them, "Clear your own city of sin and lawlessness before coming to convert us."

They stood their ground and were arrested and jailed. Some whites standing around cheered.

Among these demonstrators were twenty-one Negroes. The group included nine rabbis, eight Catholic laymen from Chicago, and forty-five Protestant clergymen. Denominations represented were Baptist, Methodist, Presbyterian, Lutheran, Protestant Episcopal, Unitarian, Disciples and United Church. Five demonstrators were Georgians. Also represented were New York, New Jersey, Massachusetts, Connecticut, Texas, Illinois, Indiana, New Hampshire and the District of Columbia.

Mrs. Malcolm E. Peabody is a slim, pretty, white-haired lady, and we use the word lady advisedly—she is the cultivated wife of a former Episcopal bishop of Central New York and the mother of Massachusetts' former governor. Few events in recent years have so pricked the conscience of church people as her arrest as a demonstrator, at age seventy-two, in St. Augustine, Florida.

In the early spring of 1964, a drive to integrate restaurants of the Southern city was in progress, and conscience told her she should go. At first officials there avoided arresting her. But finally she was picked up with the wives of two other bishops, Mrs. John Burgess (whose husband's election as first Negro bishop was recounted in Chapter 9) and Mrs. Donald Campbell, after the three women had tried to get service together. Sixteen persons were put in a cell with eight bunks, and some slept on mattresses on the floor. But Mrs. Peabody didn't complain. "I ate breakfast with my fingers—grits and little round things (sausages)," she told newsmen.

She telephoned Governor Peabody and he told her, "Mother, what is right there is right here." Another of her sons, a minister, came to visit her (she has seven grandchildren).

Arrests went up to 288. But segregation did not crumble suddenly because of the demonstration. Fifteen rabbis later were arrested for trying to integrate restaurants. Integrationists tried "dive-ins" to desegregate pools and were driven out by administration of more chemicals. Though sympathizers with the Negro were called "agitators" and "carpetbaggers," one of the leaders of the segregationists was a high-powered preacher who had come all the way from California.

The split meantime over integration in the churches of St. Augustine was nothing short of tragic. An integrated group was turned away from Grace Methodist on Easter, but the Rev. John Gill, pastor, later welcomed eight Negroes to a service. The minister of First Methodist wanted an open policy, but his parishioners overruled him and had an integrated group arrested.

In Trinity Church of Mrs. Peabody's denomination, ushers locked the door against Negroes Sunday after Sunday. But one morning the Rev. Charles Seymour, who was already in hot water with segregationists for assailing the Ku Klux Klan and defending the National Council of Churches, interrupted the service to walk down the aisle. He unlocked the front door, and in stepped a mixed group of Negroes and whites. The vestry wanted to fire him. But that was up to the bishop, and his bishop had given the OK for unlocking the door. The vestrymen couldn't get him to resign; some of them began walking out of services, however, or ostracized him socially. "I feel cold stares," Father Seymour said. And he sighed: "To think it would come to this."

The main sign of hope in St. Augustine was that in midsummer the Florida governor appointed a four-man committee to mediate the crisis there.

Describing her involvement in the city and her willingness to return for trial when the time came, Mrs. Peabody told old friends in her former upstate New York home that she had tried to follow the scripture, "Obey God rather than man."

"I found that in the South they do not feel you are really sincere unless you are willing to witness by going to jail," she said.

"I've had very touching letters from people who had given up hope."

How did it feel to be in a mixed group of activists?

"We began to feel that we were black and to look at whites askance," she said.

Their Negro companion, Mrs. Burgess, told them she had felt that her skin color was a sin. "We felt our sin was color too—white color," said Mrs. Peabody.

The bishop's wife warned that Christians must work for integration; otherwise "the Birchers or Communists" will take over and there will be interracial violence.

"There's a lot that women can do," she said. "I tell them to get active—to expose themselves. Make friends with Negroes and then hear what they say."

Support civil rights organizations, learn about race, keep talking it over, she urged.

"This is a revolution that's going on," she said with a twinkle, "and you don't want to miss it."

Agitation merged dramatically with political action in the church-backed vote-drive during the summer of 1964 in Mississippi and elsewhere in the South. One notes too how often churchmen were involved in the political activities discussed in Chapter 2, culminating in the successful drive for passage of the new civil rights law.

Social action is as important as political, and individual as well as group action has a place. When a church or church members help a Negro into a better job or aid a Negro family to find a home in an integrated area, they are promoting peaceful change and, meantime, are educating themselves and others about race relations.

Some church-related projects are out-and-out educational. The Chicago City Missionary Society, for example, noted that the city's schools lacked materials about Negro history and culture, although slightly more than half their pupils are Negro. So the society got Negro historians and teachers to develop such materials for use with the thousand children in its integrated summer program.

In spite of rioting in New York, a summer reading club

continued in 1964 for 280 Harlem children at the Presbyterian Church of the Master. About 150 adult volunteers served as tutors. Two out of three of them were white, and the coordinator, the Rev. Edward B. Fiske, was also white. These teachers kept on after the riot, said Mr. Fiske, because they realized "it is important to show that all of Harlem is not the wrong end of a night stick or a riot helmet and that there are people who are concerned about this community."

Another hopeful project, the Emergency Summer Youth Program, was started in Harlem and in the riot area of Brooklyn. More than 600 teen-agers—including some who were in the riots—worked at $1.50 an hour painting and cleaning half a dozen churches. The program coordinator, the Rev. H. Carl McCall, said it provided "constructive alternatives to violence." The project was supported by $112,000 contributed by foundations and church groups. Before the riots, requests for funds had been mostly ignored. Said an aide ruefully: "We have learned that it pays to have a riot occasionally."

Integrated projects that educate the Negro in these ways help him to find a dignified place in society more easily. But it is whites who have the real need for education, and various plans for exchanges of pulpits and congregations and home visits are aimed at helping whites to get to know Negroes as people. These projects, which have been tried for years, and which have to be carefully administered in order not to seem patronizing, have a real use in building or maintaining cables across the chasm between the races.

After the New York riots in the summer of 1964, for example, visits by Lutheran families to eight churches in the riot areas were planned, so that prayers for the white community could be asked. "We want to show that there is unity in Christ that violence cannot obscure," explained the Rev. Richard J. Neuhaus, chairman of the Lutheran Human

Relations Association. Catholic Charities and St. James Pro-Cathedral sponsored a similar person-to-person project in Brooklyn, and middle-income Irish visited low-income Negro homes a few blocks away.

Such home visits had been tried on a large scale already in a "pilgrimage of understanding" in Chicago. Some 1,500 white Protestants, Catholics and Jews visited more than 450 Negro families and talked about common problems of home and children. The aim of the visits in both Chicago and New York, of course, was to start building personal relationships across race lines; as one participant told another, "If I see you again, we have something to talk about—it's a start."

Years before in Cambridge, Massachusetts, a white Baptist church and a Negro Baptist church had tried a pilot project of joining in Sunday worship. It proved so successful that they went on holding two Sunday evening worship services together each month. Said one pastor: "We accept each other as human beings."

In the midwest, four Methodist churches began a project to "reach over the racial wall in Christian love." Two were white churches of the Iowa Conference, and two were Kansas City churches of the Central (Negro) Jurisdiction. The pastors of each pair exchanged residences and all pastoral functions for three weeks.

Another approach was that of the American Baptists in Chicago. They moved Northern Theological Seminary to a new location and converted the old campus into interracial homes for the aging.

One of the obvious advantages of the integrated local church is the opportunity for cultural education. An example of how well this can work out is the First English Church (Lutheran) of Sacramento, California. In 1956, the congregation moved into a neighborhood that was integrating fast.

By 1959, eighteen Negroes had joined the church and in two more years, the number was up to thirty-eight. Negro young people joined the Luther League.

But the real start in interracial understanding was being made with the little youngsters in vacation Bible school. One summer they studied five different countries, and the pupils were of three different backgrounds—African, Oriental, and Caucasian.

What we have been talking about in this section is largely news of the sixties, and as long as racial advance within the church is news, it is clear that segregation and inequality are the warp and woof of the fabric. "Firsts" are a reminder of beginnings, and yet they are hopeful, colorful threads.

They remind us that it is too easy to libel churches and churchmen. The chief executive officer of the United Presbyterian Church in the U.S.A., Dr. Eugene Carson Blake, commented that it was tragic that it's "still news when Christians begin to behave as they speak." Yet it is good that there is news that some churchmen do practice what they preach, and they do lead.

While the church is leaven in society, then these progressive leaders are the leaven within the leaven. They work slowly—no doubt too slowly—to change the whole.

At its best, the position of these forward-looking Christians may be compared to that of the "confessing" churchmen of Nazi Germany who opposed Hitler. These Germans tried to stand against racism—again, perhaps not enough and not soon enough. Later they preached repentance as the road to renewed vitality for their distressed churches. So too, out of struggle for brotherhood and in repentance for weakness and failures, American churchmen may find renewal for their faith and their nation.

PART FIVE

STRUGGLE OF VALUES

13 · Religious Realities

> On sweltering summer days and crisp autumn mornings, I have looked at her (America's) beautiful churches with their lofty spires pointing heavenward. . . . Over and over again I have found myself asking: "What kind of people worship here? Who is their God?"
>
> —Martin Luther King Jr.

Who is to blame for the plight of the Negro? Where does the guilt lie? The answer seems obvious—the majority has the responsibility for suffering by a minority. Yet the question of responsibility is complex. The psychiatrist sees one meaning of guilt in the psyche, and the theologian another meaning of sin in the soul. Our common sense tells us that we have to find some truth about our responsibility; otherwise we can't grasp the meaning of the Negro Revolution.

How does one react to guilt for a monstrous social evil? We know something of how, Negroes and whites alike, we reacted to the horrendous sins of exterminations in concentration camps, and the annihilations of Hiroshima and Nagasaki. We denied their magnitude. And when the insistent facts penetrated, we tried to force them out of our minds with a kind of willful amnesia. So with society's sin against the Negro. We who are white simply do not let ourselves believe the depth or extent of the suffering.

The writers of this book were deeply shocked recently when we heard whites at a church meeting say that nothing prevented a Negro's moving where he liked. This seemed to be said in all sincerity, though anyone who knows any Negro who has tried to move in our city, as in most American cities, is aware that he faces countless hurdles.

Similarly, a famous Northern editor, refusing to relate the bombing deaths of the four little Negro girls in Birmingham to conditions in his own city, wrote scathingly that no one could prove comparable Negro tragedies occurred in his community. Yet his greenest reporter could have turned up evidence to prove that deaths from disease and malnutrition and fires are regularly higher in Northern ghettoes than outside. The segregation of colored people, who are in effect swept under the ghetto rug of the city, abets white indifference. And the whites, ignorant of these conditions by choice, can assuage guilt by saying there is nothing to be guilty about!

Whites also avoid facing their blame by contending that the Negro is to blame. It seems incredible that a majority could claim that a minority is responsible for its own sufferings in a society controlled by the majority. This is the meaning, however, of the now somewhat dated contention that the Negro is inferior—so he must be to blame for his lot. And if it is no longer sophisticated to speak of inferiority, then one speaks of the cultural deprivation of the Negro, which suggests that when he has brought his children up to the cultural level of whites, then they may study in schools with privileged (that is, superior) white children.

Another oblique way of blaming the Negro is the insistence that Negroes ought to study and work hard instead of agitating, which suggests that laziness and not society is holding them down. Likewise, when whites challenge Negro leaders to lift or control or push their Negro followers, the implication is that Negro society is to blame.

When Negro violence breaks out in Detroit or Harlem or a Mississippi town, white leaders hasten to warn Negroes that their cause is being set back. They rarely call upon whites to examine their own instigation of such violence. Even when whites burn Negro churches or chase Negroes with ax handles or electric prods, white racists allege that Negroes have incited the violence. It is as if, at every point, whites are eager to exonerate themselves by saying: "Ah-ha, you see, you Negroes, it is your laziness or ignorance or barbarism that is really responsible for your suffering, not our white society!"

Paradoxically, though, there is a way in which the Negroes share blame, and that is their desire to cast all blame on whites. Since there is something salutary in taking blame repentantly on oneself, it is healthy when the white citizen examines himself and sees his fault, and the Negro rightly aids him to see his responsibility. But if the Negro self-righteously excludes Negroes from all guilt simply because they are black, he errs. Many individual Negroes may conduct themselves in a way that is blameless, as do individual whites—that is, to the degree that blamelessness in such a situation is possible—but every subculture in social conflict also has individuals who are guilty. This fact creates the dilemma the Negro and the white liberal face when they try to make the defense of "it's wrong—but" for Negro excesses; for example, "It is wrong for Negroes to riot and loot, but the brutalities of white policemen have made it inevitable." Despite the elements of truth in the assertion, it does not remove all stigma from the guilty Negroes, since many other members of their race who have suffered equally have maintained a high level of conduct.

There is a sense, however, in which all whites are to blame. It is the nature of corporate sins, such as wars and racism and exploitation and genocides, that all in a society share in the guilt.

We must ask ourselves what we are doing to prevent the race explosions of 1970. For some, the answer is "nothing." Others of us are doing something. But none of us can perhaps do enough.

This is the tragic weight of the phrase "too little, too late." Negroes have been marking time for over a century. In the early sixties, many looked forward to 1963, the centenary of the Emancipation Proclamation, hoping for freedom at last. But the months go by and slip into years, and change comes, but very slowly. When anger and frustration bring an explosion, we are all to blame.

We three Negro professional women who had been invited to address a United Church Women's group had talked frankly about the problem of poor self-image that plagues the Negro because of the way whites have structured America. The women wanted to know what they could do.

Make a "subtlety search," we suggested—find hidden bigotry. Disappointment registered on many faces. Surely Our City does not have many of these hidden prejudices?

We discovered that this meeting on "Assignment: Race" and one other were the only ones the UCW had held during the year which had not been covered by photographers for the evening newspaper. The other occasion had also featured a Negro woman speaker.

Later I made a point of questioning a local Negro leader; he had been told by one of the newspaper's editors that it was a policy not to use pictures of Negro women on the women's pages. Something about protecting white woman-

hood! Pictures of Negro engaged girls and brides were never used, he said.

The church women thought they had accomplished something by having Negroes speak. This had been the final year of a three-year study on race, and one sensed that some of the women felt that the problem was nearly solved! Yet right under their noses was a glaring indication that race as a badge of inferiority was still very much present.

Here is the type of subtlety that UCW could bring pressure to remove, since UCW in that city represents nearly every white church. Printing Negro brides' pictures would boost the feelings of self-worth of many young women. It would also say a great deal to the whites, unused to thinking of Negroes as having the same dreams and fulfilments as they.

Whatever else the UCW does, it should boycott the newspapers and let the editors know white women need not be "protected" from Negro women.

A real commitment to such actions should be the goal of white Christians, not just having Negroes visit churches on Sunday. What a change could result from such commitments! As whites began to ferret out subtleties, they would begin to see the implications of being a Negro in America.

As blame, sin and guilt make up one cluster of factors contributing to interracial tensions, the emotions of love and hate also comprise a pair of religious realities involved in the conflict. In America's past there has never been much really mature love between individuals of the black and white races. Though many Southerners insist they love Negroes, the affection is apt to be similar to the feeling they have for their hounds and horses. On the other hand, few persons except those with emotional problems have felt active hatred. Indifference probably best describes the traditional attitude of the white toward his Negro brethren, and resignation to his lot has been the most common Negro emotion; he has often been too enervated to generate real hate.

But all that is changing. The beginnings of integration have stirred the possibility of equality and loosed the potentiality of hatred. Norman Thomas, the Socialist leader, used to say that revolutions did not come from the really depressed but from those a cut above, who had hope and resentments and vigor. Today the Negro has attained enough to want the revolution that will take him the whole way: *Freedom Now!* Those who would block it or slow it are naturally seen as hateful.

Much of the new Negro hatred is inarticulate. Negro intellectuals like James Baldwin have given voice to it, but the white man never quite believes that a novelist can speak for the porter or charwoman who represents "Negro" to his mind. The Black nationalists and Muslims stir hatred, but again the white man wants to believe that their cries are the excesses of extremists. Civil rights leaders and ministers like Martin Luther King Jr. warn of the hate that is rising, and the white man nods piously, again not quite believing. When there is an irrational demonstration or a blind riot, the white man may be shocked into seeing the face of hate. But he is more apt to see what he considers only a Negro lack of appreciation, barbarism and excessive demands. A reporter, going into the riot area of Rochester, New York, was shocked when Negroes taunted him: "We hate you, white boy! Why don't you tell our part of the story?"

The problem is that Negroes and whites do not know each other. The Negro knows the white man largely as an autocratic lord saying, "Boy." The white man knows the Negro largely as a servant or subordinate. This has changed somewhat in the last generation, of course. In a host of committees and societies and church groups and other organizations, some contrived and some now quite natural, whites have become acquainted with "the better class" of Negroes. Too many white doctors still know no Negro doctors, too many white professors know no Negro professors, too many white clerks and firemen know no Negro clerks and firemen still; but a great many ministers and factory workers and teachers and social workers of both races do know their counterparts.

One part of the problem, therefore, is to increase the number of contacts across racial lines and reduce the degree of not-knowingness. The next step is to get a real flow and exchange of insights and ideas and attitudes back and forth.

Separation is still the major obstacle. In the South the philosophy of "separate but equal" has made a virtue of separatism. In the North, with its growing but often superficial integration in the last half century, the psychological separatism has been as real as in the South. The arguments for separatism, of course, have ranged all the way from "Negroes really like it better that way" on to the ultimate bugaboo of miscegenation. Sometimes one wonders, however, whether the ultimate bulwark of separatism is not a subconscious fear on the part of the white that if he gets any closer to the Negro, he will be in a position to feel the full emotional thrust of Negro hurt and resentment and suffering and hate.

For as separatism breaks down, more than love and kindness are communicated. It is this knowledge that creates the intransigence of the South African and of the White Citizens Council member—fear of the hate that will break out if the thumb screw is loosened only a tiny bit. The risk that the white man has to take is that as freedom comes he can still, with minimum damage, absorb the hate of the decades—that men can let the wound cleanse itself and then start over with goodwill.

One Negro writer has said that whites are obsessed with the question of whether the black man hates or loves them and asks: "Why don't you settle for indifference?" Indifference is better than hate, to be sure. But indifference has been the sinful stance of the white man, sinful because no man has a right to ignore his brother.

White hate and indifference have sown a sufficient whirlwind already. Negro hate will bring more white hate; Negro indifference will bring more white indifference. The greatest Negro preachers of nonviolence have reiterated that Negroes must try to find love and help the whites respond.

Two religious questions that bear on the race problem are: Who is man? And what is his proper attitude toward other men?

Since the development of the theory of evolution there have been hard-line thinkers who have felt that the strong have a natural right to what they can get, and if the weak are swept aside into misery and despair, too bad—that is the Nature of the Universe. But Christ said to feed the hungry and clothe the naked. That, says the so-called social Darwinist, is soft Christianity, which would coddle and preserve the unfit. The idea has had a resurgence in recent years: the word "freedom" is often misinterpreted as the prerogative of the strong to deny to the depressed that other democratic right, equality.

Gov. Ross Barnett has declared "the self-evident proposition" that the races can never be equal. Arguing from this premise, the racist assumes that since the Negro is less than the white, then he cannot be made in the image of God; this makes him less than human—that is, subhuman.

Link up the brutalitarian social theory of the hard-line

evolutionist and the superiority complex of the die-hard segregationist and you have a philosophy, vicious and non-Christian, that justifies leaving colored people in degradation.

If man is his brother's keeper, however, how can a Christian abandon Negroes to the rigorous "natural selection" of poverty and disease? If the Negro is fully human and is made in the image of God, moreover, how can one deny him equal part in the common life? We who are white Christians probably do not have the stomach to repress Negroes violently—nor have we the rigor to repel their violence if, accepting the tooth-and-claw theory, they turn to gunpowder. Our only alternative to repression and violence, therefore, is massive cooperation and reformation.

Many naive whites insist that things are going along well between the races. As an Italian-American youth told a New York reporter when Negroes "invaded" what he considered "his" section of Manhattan: "We were getting along fine with the niggers until this thing happened." But "fine," of course, is defined here in white terms. A young CORE friend of ours reflects: " 'Everything was fine until you got started,' they say. But we'd never have gotten started if everything had been fine."

Believing that Negro agitation has caused interracial tension, rather than white suppression, is the tragic error of the thoughtless. So backlash results. But backlash is bigotry; the only thing that is new about bigotry is that it is now open, and that surprises only other whites—the Negroes have known that it was there all along. If the Negro reveals his frustrations, the white will reveal his basic recalcitrance to change. As Dick Gregory has pointed out, civil rights demonstrations are like a check for cancer, and they're simply bringing out the cancer.

To carry on the analogy, the cancer will not be cured by

sending away the doctor. It will not be cured if the Negroes simply give up their struggle—an unlikely possibility! For it was white bigotry that caused suppression—that finally caused Negro revolt—that has unmasked the bigotry. There is even reason to rejoice at the backlash, for it means Negroes are getting through to whites. It reveals that the staid white community has at last been confronted with the necessity for action. The price is anxiety, but at least the whites are no longer enjoying a cozy psychosis of unreality.

The goods and bads of today's racial conflict are all interwoven in a crazy-patterned social fabric—demands for better jobs and schools, white condescension, bad housing, police brutality, riots, demonstrations. There is also a pattern of cause and effect. You can't have discrimination without a Negro reaction. You can't have backlash without counter-backlash. Segregation must produce its result, unrest.

The only cure is to eradicate segregationist attitudes. They can find no moral sustenance in democratic or Christian truths; they must go. Other attitudes, of respect and cooperation, must be put in their place, and that is where the church comes in.

14 · A White Revolution

Christian people need to be made aware of the moral and spiritual dimensions of the problem of race relations. The creation of a new pattern of race relations requires a long, long effort based on Christianity and American patriotism. White people must be *converted*.

—Eugene Carson Blake

The real stone wall that restrains the Negro revolution is made up not only of the rocks of prejudice and backlash but of the very bricks of our industrial society. We are in an era when conformist "team-workers" get ahead. This is the reason for our professed concern about "the organization man" and "status seekers"—and there are more white Uncle Toms than black. Moreover, the threat to the soul of the American churches has long been the temptation to be merely respectable social clubs where men improve their status. So the interracial movement, which seeks to strengthen individual black men in vigorous nonconformity and to reshape our genteel churches into cells of reform, is deeply radical in the purest sense of that word.

The nub of the Christian problem is that the church today is a most flimsy instrument for revolution. Christians—the white ones—are inclined to like things as they are. Inducing them to help reshape our society to a decent interracial structure is only one part of the immense task of converting them to the need for regenerating the whole world.

Right now the struggle appears to be going against the rabid segregationists, who are being cut off in their "strategic hamlets." But there is one grand strategy with which they could delay the revolution.

Separate the illiterate, explosive mass of Negroes from the middle-class Negroes who have begun to see hope; cut them both off from the seasoned leadership that has slowly developed since World War II; widen the rivalries among the rights organizations by encouraging individual power grabs; increase the mistrust of all Negroes for the white liberal who knows that political advance is made by skillful compromise, even in the area of inalienable rights; encourage secular liberals and church social-actionists to discredit each other; separate all active integrationists from the white moderates who must help to make up any continuing political majority in a democracy—split, fragment and divide all the coalition of factions and parties that can aid the depressed black people, and the segregationists can hang on awhile longer. Blinded by their phobia about a mythical Communist conspiracy controlling the race movement, the die-hards are probably too unwitting to conspire effectively to such a victory. But the fighters for equality, if they do not avoid divisiveness, may do the job for them.

Every thoughtful American Negro knows that it is the "good whites"—inadequate as they may be—who hold the key to his future hopes, simply because there are more whites than blacks. He must cooperate with whites. And the "good whites" must act, but not necessarily all in the same way. Each must find the level of activity that squares with his conscience and temperament. Each must think through the values on which he will act.

What are the values that should motivate American religious people, both Negro and white?

Because of racial status, the values of Negroes and whites differ in some respects. Many of the Negro's goals are selfish, in the sense that he is seeking his own needs. Often, the Negro asserts that he is not really interested in living among whites or sending his children to white schools or going to church with whites—he just wants the good things which, in America, are normally associated with the white community.

Such goals may be criticized as middle-class. The religious leader may attack them as essentially materialistic. While such contentions contain truth, it hardly behooves the white intellectual who enjoys inside-plumbing and regular garbage collections and a television set to attack the "bourgeois values" of the Negro family that wants the same.

In a midde-class society, what other turn can a fight for equality take? Equality means equal rights and equal values. The goals of bringing better food and decent houses and medical care to the people of underprivileged countries are also in a sense materialistic and bourgeois; yet we recognize the validity of such goals.

Moreover, since our measures of injustice are mostly physical, any struggle for justice becomes mixed up with materialism. Our criticisms of communists are in part directed against the strictures they place on speech and religion, but we also condemn the barriers they raise to prevent individuals from moving as they want, having their own homes, and buying and selling as they please. Our founding fathers had their material goals in breaking with Great Britain; there is no real inconsistency between wanting to rid oneself of taxes to improve a business situation and in seeking the wider freedoms. It is natural that the Negro struggle against injustice should be expressed as a struggle for freedom against restrictions, the liberty to move and buy and sell and improve himself materially.

This is not to say that the Negro is never motivated unselfishly. Ironically, it seems that when he is most unselfish, he is most attacked. Whites seem to be able to understand a man when he fights for his own well-being but not when he fights for someone else's improvement. The Northern Negro has no run-ins with the white community if he seeks improvement while "keeping his place"; but if he idealistically goes to Mississippi to help fellow Negroes register to vote, he becomes an interfering carpetbagger.

A race or an individual can have both materialistic and idealistic aspirations. Such mixed motives are obvious enough in a white man. Why not in the Negro? The questions are: Where do you put your emphasis? What do you do when your goals seem to conflict? Negroes have to make a decision as to whether they should back better housing projects even if they are segregated or accept poorer houses that have the advantage, from the Christian viewpoint, of being in an integrated area. They must decide whether to accept ghetto-type schools if they are promised better instruction, or allow their children to undergo the difficulty of bussing to distant schools, in order to enjoy a more cosmopolitan education for an integrated American society. The "good" white can be an especially deceptive friend when he appeals to the Negro's selfish side, urging him to accept materialistic betterment on the "separate but equal" pattern, within the framework of a segregated, undemocratic structure.

On the white side, there is a similar struggle of materialistic and idealistic values. The problem of race confronts the white man constantly with the need of weighing values.

Today, most whites would probably agree that there are values in integration. There is at least the value that integration is the legal way, since the civil rights law was approved. But many and perhaps most whites would go further. In their hearts they recognize the justice of integration. They agree that Negroes should have the right to better education and jobs.

The problem comes when those values are set against other values. Honesty is a fine goal until one sees the dollars that can be gained by a bit of dishonesty. And so the values of racial justice and equality are more easily praised in isolation. When they are set against the other convictions white Americans hold, it gets sticky.

There are first of all the phony values.

It may seem incredible that anyone calling himself a Christian would reject a real value, such as fairness to the Negro, to accept a false one. But it happens constantly.

What are these false gods? For one, personal exclusiveness, based on false notions, that Negroes smell differently, or are "naturally immoral" (although they are also supposed to be more religious!). A bit of serious investigation and thought will demonstrate the falsity of such ideas to the fair-minded white person.

A value that is phony in a subtler way is the idea of racial superiority. This is a particularly deceptive notion when it is grandly conceded that the Negro may not *really* be inferior; but given his bad housing and his poor education and his limited cultural background and all, he *is* inferior after all. So the white can blandly say that "that kind" of Negro should not live near him and "that kind" of Negro child is not good enough for a white school. The value of integration goes out the window as phony Aryan values are exalted.

Another phony value is property protectiveness, based on the idea that property values go down when Negroes move into any area. Careful studies show that this is not true.

Real estate men can be quoted to prove that Negroes actually pay more, unit for like unit, than whites. Yet the false idea on property values is still used as a reason why the white person does not follow through on his firm verbalizing about integration. His misguided selfishness takes over.

A much more difficult contrast of values confronts the white when he sees that the segregated status quo does have real values.

The dedicated extremist against segregation may contend there are no such values. But what he is really arguing is that, compared to the values of an integrated society, they are minuscule. That is true, but they do exist.

There is, for example, a value in maintaining American schools for those in the neighborhood. There is a value in spending school money for better teachers instead of for bus drivers to end *de facto* segregation. There is a value in getting more housing for the poor, even if the political forces insist that it be segregated. Since unquestionably some Negroes are warped personalities, there is value in "segregating" those individuals from residential areas (though admittedly white criminal elements can't readily be segregated from those areas, and Negro parents also don't want to raise families close to such people).

These are lesser values than brotherhood. But such values do exist, and it is not realistic to act as if they will not be weighed by whites. They are being weighed all the time, and integration is not always tipping the balance. As the white tries to understand the Negro restlessness, the Negro must try to understand these factors that make the white hesitate. The values of the status quo make well-meaning whites use that phrase that infuriates the Negro: "Some of my best friends are Negroes but . . . ." What the well-meaning white may really be saying, if the Negro will listen is:

"Some of my best friends are Negroes, and I want Negroes for friends, and I really believe in integration—but there are other values in my life today which I want to keep and which I have to weigh."

From the Christian point of view, the white may make the wrong choice as he weighs. He may exalt the lesser values. But the task of the integrationist is to understand the real values in the status quo as well as the phony, and get people to look at them seriously up against their deepest convictions of democracy and religion.

There are then, finally, the outright selfish values. They are masked values—first cousins of prejudice. They are real in the sense that they certainly exist as values dearly held by many Americans, but they are phony in the sense that they are false gods. They are unidealistic, anti-spiritual, unchristian. But since we call ours a Christian society, they of course are not so labeled openly and blatantly. They are screened, hidden.

What are these masked values? They are the values of status and self-exaltation. They are the values that provide cheap domestic help when Negro women are kept ignorant. They help the white industrialist maintain a pool of cheap labor, and they help the white union member get higher monopoly prices for labor with a segregated organization. They support the block-busting realtor who profits from myths about Negro housing. They flatter the ego of the ignorant white whose only claim to status is his pink skin.

It is these selfish masked values that our communities may promote. Individual human beings may show compassion; this is especially true when the individual white deals, not with abstract "Negroes," but with an individual colored man. But in the aggregate men fall easily to their lowest common denominator: "moral men and immoral society."

So we have the basis for the cruelties of what is now much spoken of as "the power structure." In their social and political roles of leadership, otherwise good Christians make decisions and set courses of action that maintain the status quo in race relations. They "don't want to upset the boat." And the status quo means the hardening of present values that shut the Negro out.

Nothing is gained by pretending that this idolatry of selfishness is not widespread. There is an ideological conflict between the Children of Light and the Children of Darkness. It is ancient and it is worldwide, and in the United States our minority groups are in the middle of it.

On the one side is the democratic ideal of equality. On the other is the yearning of the status-seekers, the lust for a status quo that provides a ladder of bowed backs on which the greediest can climb fastest.

On the one side is the ideal of brotherhood. On the other is worry about riches, called "property values."

On the one side is Christian love—*agape*. On the other is wealth and grasping power.

None of us, of course, is perfectly on the side of love and brotherhood. White and Negro alike, we are dyed in various shades of sinful selfishness.

But there *are* the shades. The Negro creates an unreal world when he talks and acts as if all whites are equally guilty of prejudice. They aren't. And whites do the integration cause no good when they too, in masochistic confessional, blur the distinctions between the prejudiced and the unprejudiced. There are, notwithstanding ambiguities, Children of Light.

Once the Christian has thought through the conflict of values and false gods, what action can he take?

We put the question to Dr. Eugene Carson Blake, the

Presbyterian leader who also is chairman of the National Council's Commission on Religion and Race. Here are his succinct suggestions:

—Desegregate the churches themselves wherever there is a Negro community to make it possible.

—Create social opportunities for contacts between whites and Negroes.

—Become part of community effort to take rapid steps in the following areas of concern in each community—community by community:

1. Equality before the law.
2. Job opportunity.
3. Educational opportunity.
4. Fair housing.
5. Public accommodations and public dignity.

"What about demonstrations?" we asked.

"Demonstrations are simply a means to make the white power structure listen to reason and to act," he said. "Reconciliation is the end and the best means of Christians. But demonstration with and behind Negro leaders is still required in many situations."

Did he feel Negro Christians should do anything specifically?

"Carry on responsibly as they have behind their excellent leadership," he replied.

So much emphasis has been placed on civil rights that leadership of the Negro's struggle of decency has become synonymous with leadership for Negro advancement. The Negro looks to the civil rights leaders as his leaders, but unless they declare themselves loudly and clearly on economic, educational, social and other situations affecting Negroes, they should openly limit themselves to civil rights issues.

Communication about ways the Negro can improve himself has been hampered by the fact that whites use any shortcomings of the Negroes as an excuse for their own prejudices. If they learn that some Negroes are "color struck"—that is, more inclined toward their lighter brothers and sisters—this becomes justification for their own prejudices toward Negroes. It does not occur to whites that their attitudes—as illustrated by the fact that a Negro chosen as a "first" for a position is almost invariably light—cause the Negro's attitudes.

There is a risk in commenting on Negro obligations. But if these realities are not faced, the Negro will always be twenty years behind the whites in terms of his earnings, life style and achievements.

Recently a CORE chapter sponsored a meeting to air 108 specific suggestions. To make the proposals more meaningful, deprived Negroes described their plight and literally begged for help. One speaker told of a family with twelve children living in a three-bedroom apartment, and of her own struggle to get more living space as her family expanded from three to six children during her six years in public housing. But to expect public housing authorities to keep up with the population explosion is to adopt a "give me" approach.

From this meeting and observation, two musts on the part of Negroes should be emphasized: (1) birth control and (2) more information on economic and educational matters that will help the Negro get a better grip on life. In view of the cost of a college education, how does a Negro family with ten, twelve, or more children expect to give them the proper start in life? What landlord wants his property overrun by many children? Parents of over-large families are unable to take their children to places of cultural enrichment.

I think Negro leaders should lead here. They must pro-claim loudly and clearly that, now that opportunities are rapidly opening, parents must be as concerned with child-launching as with child-bearing. That would be "pro-phetic" leadership. Negro leaders must gain this stature, or the civil rights struggle and the poor will be with us always. In short, there must also be a revolution in the leadership thinking of the Negro Revolution.

The questions of rights and brotherhood come down to a question of individual commitment. One organization that has demonstrated the meaning of commitment is the Wo-men's Intergroup Committee in Providence, Rhode Island. The WICs—their symbol is a lighted candle!—have grown to 350 members as they have worked to break through the barriers among ethnic and religious groups in their state. Said one: "We wanted to do more than just meet once or twice a year, or during Brotherhood Week, then return to our separate social lives."

So they acted. They sponsored living-room study groups of husbands and wives—secretaries, professors, postal clerks, brokers and housewives. They got 10,000 to sign pledges to welcome minority groups to their neighborhoods.

With this kind of yeast, it was logical that in Rhode Island a group of Christians and Jews should prepare a "call for commitment to racial justice in churches and syna-gogues" for an interfaith conference at Providence. One of the best phases of this was a statement urging individuals to make a personal commitment. Here are some parts of the suggested pledge:

I commit myself to act with love, with charity, with under-standing and with courage, and to honor the essential dignity and equality of all men, under one God, because we are the sons of one father, and therefore brothers.

I commit myself to working for the adoption and implementation of a Commitment to Racial Justice in my own church or synagogue . . . .

I commit myself to work for racial integration in my own community, neighborhood and school.

I commit myself in my profession or business to instituting and enforcing non-discriminatory employment and promotion policies . . . .

I commit myself to building interpersonal friendships across racial lines . . . .

Fourteen commitments in all were suggested.

Individual Christians may, by examining their consciences, think of such commitments they themselves could make, that they must make, in groups or as individuals. What a difference in race relations would quickly come if everyone who calls himself a Christian would act on his conscientious convictions. As a new Episcopal bishop, the Rt. Rev. Ned Cole Jr., has said: "One person on a school board, in a PTA meeting . . . one person who sells real estate . . . one person who controls money or public policy . . . may by his involvement and moral persuasion set in motion a chain of events as effective as Branch Rickey's employment of Jackie Robinson."

Each of us, white and Negro, can commit himself to use whatever talents he has in the struggle of decency. Members of the United Church Women in Syracuse have been conducting for almost two years an "each one teach one" literacy program to reach thousands, half of them Negroes. Their commitment is evident in their lack of condescension toward those with lower income.

Sometimes commitment is individual. A good example is an advertising artist at a Syracuse department store. She quietly "integrated" her drawings of fashion models used in daily newspaper ads, so that now Negro faces appear

*in ads for Father's Day sportswear and for "Back to School"
clothes. In such efforts, the Protestant belief that every
vocation is a Christian calling finds a new dimension.*

To oversimplify, there are two kinds of white Americans
today. Some want change on the race front. Some don't.

Those who don't want change want the status quo. When
they say we can't change society overnight, they usually
mean they don't want it to change at all. They don't like
uppity Negroes. They recall the good old days when a
Negro and his betters had good relations—like that of a
first-class serf and his lord. They want to "protect" what
they have—property values, white jobs, white schools, white
churches.

For whites who do want change in racial relations, there
is no middle ground. You're either for integration or you're
against it, as the CORE leaders say—no one is on the side-
lines. "He who is not for us is against us."

But because of the superior social status which the white
has, there is an uncomfortable and almost inevitable
noblesse oblige about his attitude toward the Negro. He
escapes the sense of condescension with difficulty. Unless
he does escape it, he may seem at worst like an unctuous
Lady Bountiful giving a Thanksgiving basket, or at best
like an aristocratic Tolstoy trying to assuage his conscience
by being brotherly to peasants. Sensing this difficulty of
genuine friendship between two individuals as equals across
racial lines, the Negro may feel that he sees white hypocrisy
everywhere.

In a way he is right. But there is an error in judging hypocrisy as the ultimate fault. The White Citizens Council
member is the most unhypocritical white: he makes no
bones about his desire for the status quo of 1900. Any white
who is not an out-and-out racist must struggle constantly

against the brainwashing to which society has subjected him from birth. Unconscious reservations may cause him to withhold complete commitment to immediate and full integration even when he believes he has no prejudice. Or he may lack the courage fully to oppose his racist neighbors. The Negro has to muster what he can of his traditionally vaunted patience to tolerate the various shades of hypocrisy. The white in turn can reduce his hypocrisy only by increasing the vigor of his commitment.

In the worldwide ideological conflict of the compassionate and the bigoted, the Children of Light can win only by such increased commitment to the good of all men.

The Negro, as he insists on his own individual rights, must recognize the indivisibility of the struggle—of his need to support his colored compatriot in the next block, the next state, the next county.

For the white, as we have suggested, the demand that racial justice makes on him is even more overwhelming because he must reconcile conflicting values in his heart. Where phony values tempt him, he has to examine the issues honestly. Where selfish values draw him, he has to renounce them. Where some genuinely good objectives conflict with the high values of integration, he has to weigh and ponder prayerfully.

By frankly insisting on the status quo, a white may avoid the charge of hypocrisy on the race question, but if he professes Christ, he is miring himself in countless religious rationalizations and hypocrisies. The white who grants that the values he holds highest are inconsistent with the subjugation of Negroes, however, can rid himself of unconscious or cowardly hypocrisy as his conscience drives him to dedicate himself wholeheartedly to the cause of equality and brotherhood.

The struggle of decency and for decency is an all-out one.

Where lukewarmness is an abomination, each Christian has to commit himself. Such dedication of whites is the absolute prerequisite to racial peace with justice. For our problem is not really a Negro problem, of course. Progressives have known for a long time that our race problem should be called the White Problem. What America must have is a White Revolution—a revolution in attitudes and dedication and action.